First World War
and Army of Occupation
War Diary
France, Belgium and Germany

25 DIVISION
Headquarters, Branches and Services
Royal Army Ordnance Corps
Deputy Director Ordnance Services
1 April 1916 - 20 February 1919

WO95/2232/2

The Naval & Military Press Ltd
www.nmarchive.com
Published in association with The National Archives

Published by

The Naval & Military Press Ltd

Unit 10 Ridgewood Industrial Park,

Uckfield, East Sussex,

TN22 5QE England

Tel: +44 (0) 1825 749494

www.naval-military-press.com

www.nmarchive.com

This diary has been reprinted in facsimile from the original. Any imperfections are inevitably reproduced and the quality may fall short of modern type and cartographic standards.

Contents

Document type	Place/Title	Date From	Date To
Heading	WO95/2232/2 Deputy Director Ordnance Services		
Heading	25th Division Divl Troops Dep. Dir. Ordnance Services Apr 1916-Feb 1919		
Heading	25th. Div. D.A.D.O.S. April 1916 1 Feb. 19		
Heading	War Diary XXV Division April 1916		
War Diary	Roellecourt Nr St. Pol	01/04/1916	30/04/1916
Heading	25th. Div. D.A.D.O.S. May 1916.		
War Diary	Acq	06/05/1916	31/05/1916
Heading	25th. Div. D.A.D.O.S. June 1916.		
War Diary	Roellecourt	01/06/1916	16/06/1916
War Diary	Domart	17/06/1916	24/06/1916
War Diary	Canaples	25/06/1916	26/06/1916
War Diary	Rubempre	27/06/1916	29/06/1916
War Diary	Contay	30/06/1916	30/06/1916
Heading	25th. Div. D.A.D.O.S. July 1916.		
Miscellaneous	D A A & Q M G Attached Is my Diary For July 1916	01/08/1916	01/08/1916
War Diary	Henencourt	09/07/1916	11/07/1916
War Diary	Senlis	12/07/1916	18/07/1916
War Diary	Beauval	19/07/1916	20/07/1916
War Diary	Beauval Bus	22/07/1916	23/07/1916
War Diary	Bus	25/07/1916	25/07/1916
War Diary	Bertrancourt	26/07/1916	31/07/1916
Heading	25th. Div. D.A.D.O.S. August 1916.		
Miscellaneous	A.A. & Q.M.G.	01/09/1916	01/09/1916
War Diary	Bertrancourt	01/08/1916	08/08/1916
War Diary	Bus Les Artois	10/08/1916	12/08/1916
Heading	25th. Div. D.A.D.O.S. September 1916.		
Miscellaneous	D.A.A. & Q.M.G. 25th Division	30/09/1916	30/09/1916
War Diary	Senlis	01/09/1916	06/09/1916
War Diary	Acheux	07/09/1916	08/09/1916
War Diary	Doulens	10/09/1916	10/09/1916
War Diary	Bernaville	11/09/1916	11/09/1916
War Diary	Domquenr Le Plony	12/09/1916	20/09/1916
War Diary	Domquenr	21/09/1916	24/09/1916
War Diary	Boral	25/09/1916	25/09/1916
War Diary	Acheux	26/09/1916	30/09/1916
Heading	25th. Div. D.A.D.O.S. October 1916		
War Diary	Acheux	01/10/1916	01/10/1916
War Diary	Henencourt	02/10/1916	03/10/1916
War Diary	Douzincourt	04/10/1916	21/10/1916
War Diary	Contay	22/10/1916	24/10/1916
War Diary	Beauval	25/10/1916	27/10/1916
War Diary	Caestre	28/10/1916	31/10/1916
Heading	25th. Div. D.A.D.O.S. November 1916.		
War Diary	Caestre	01/11/1916	05/11/1916
War Diary	Bailleul	06/11/1916	30/11/1916
Heading	25th. Div. D.A.D.O.S. December 1916.		
Miscellaneous	Headquarters G/25th Division		
War Diary	Bailleul	01/12/1916	31/12/1916
Miscellaneous	D A A & Q M G 25th Division	02/02/1917	02/02/1917

War Diary	De Seule	01/01/1917	31/01/1917
War Diary	De Seule	01/02/1917	24/02/1917
War Diary	Caestre	25/02/1917	19/03/1917
War Diary	Merris	20/03/1917	26/03/1917
War Diary	Bailleul	27/03/1917	09/06/1917
War Diary	Ravelsburg	10/06/1917	24/06/1917
War Diary	Bomy	25/06/1917	05/07/1917
War Diary	Busseboom Area	09/07/1917	18/07/1917
War Diary	Reninghelst Area	19/07/1917	24/07/1917
War Diary	Busseboom area	25/07/1917	31/07/1917
War Diary		01/08/1917	16/08/1917
War Diary	Steenwoorde	17/08/1917	09/09/1917
War Diary	Labeuvriere	10/09/1917	06/10/1917
War Diary	Locon	07/10/1917	28/11/1917
War Diary	Bomy	29/11/1917	03/12/1917
War Diary	Achiet Le Petit Grevillers	04/12/1917	11/12/1917
War Diary	Grevillers	12/12/1917	14/12/1917
War Diary	Favreuil	15/12/1917	30/01/1918
War Diary	Sheet 59 C. H. 15c.3.6	01/02/1918	12/02/1918
War Diary	Achiet Le Petit	13/02/1918	27/03/1918
War Diary	Camples	28/03/1918	31/03/1918
Miscellaneous	A Form. Messages And Signals.	20/03/1918	20/03/1918
Miscellaneous	D.A.O.G 25th Div	21/05/1918	21/05/1918
War Diary	Merris	01/04/1918	03/04/1918
War Diary	De Seule	04/04/1918	09/04/1918
War Diary	Meteren	10/04/1918	10/04/1918
War Diary	Godwaersvelde	11/04/1918	13/04/1918
War Diary	Steenvoorde	14/04/1918	20/04/1918
War Diary	Sandylook Camp	21/04/1918	22/04/1918
War Diary	Jack Camp	23/04/1918	30/04/1918
War Diary	Houtkerke	01/05/1918	04/05/1918
War Diary	Bombecque	05/05/1918	10/05/1918
War Diary	Arcis Le Ponsart	11/05/1918	22/05/1918
War Diary	Montigny	23/05/1918	31/05/1918
War Diary	Bergeres	01/06/1918	03/06/1918
War Diary	Etoges	04/06/1918	08/06/1918
War Diary	Allemont	09/06/1918	14/06/1918
War Diary	Gleurs	15/06/1918	30/06/1918
Miscellaneous	Mitchett Camp Aldershot		
War Diary	Mitchett	01/08/1918	30/08/1918
War Diary	Antchelt Camp	01/09/1918	15/09/1918
War Diary	Boulogne St Riquer	16/09/1918	27/09/1918
War Diary	Henencourt	28/09/1918	30/09/1918
War Diary	Montauban	01/10/1918	03/10/1918
War Diary	Aenlu	04/10/1918	04/10/1918
War Diary	St Emilie	05/10/1918	09/10/1918
War Diary	Estrees	10/10/1918	18/10/1918
War Diary	Maretz	19/10/1918	25/10/1918
War Diary	Honnechy	26/10/1918	06/11/1918
War Diary	Ponereuil	07/11/1918	08/11/1918
War Diary	Landrecies	09/11/1918	13/11/1918
War Diary	Le Cateau	14/11/1918	30/11/1918
War Diary	Avesnes Les Aubert	01/12/1918	31/01/1919
Miscellaneous	The a.a & Q M G 25th Division	01/04/1919	01/04/1919
War Diary	Avesnes Les Aubert	01/02/1919	20/02/1919

WO/95/2232

/2 Deputy Director Ordnance Services

25TH DIVISION
DIVL TROOPS

DEP.DIR.ORDNANCE SERVICES

APR 1916-FEB 1919

25th. DIV. D. A. D. O. S.

A P R I L 1 9 1 6.

1

Feb. '19

D A D O S
25 DW
Vol 2

WAR DIARY

XXV DIVISION

APRIL. 1916

S Roberts Capt
D.A.D.O.S.

Army Form C. 2118.

Instructions regarding War Diaries and Intelligence Summaries are contained in F. S. Regs., Part II. and the Staff Manual respectively. Title pages will be prepared in manuscript.

WAR DIARY
or
INTELLIGENCE SUMMARY.
(Erase heading not required.)

Place	Date	Hour	Summary of Events and Information	Remarks and references to Appendices
ROELLECOURT Nr ST. POL	1 4/16		Quarterly Return of Bulk Issues sent to A.D.O.S.	
			Dump visited by Col. Moulton Barrett D.D.O.S. & General Parsons. D.O.S. Everything satisfactory.	
	2 4/16		Preparations made for opening a Divisional School at Buneville.	
	3 4/16		Routine – visited 2 Units, everything satisfactory.	
			Arrangements made for return of Winter Clothing commencing 6th inst. with first Group.	
			D.O's put in for Board of Survey to be arranged for disposal of unserviceable articles.	
	4 4/16		Divisional Shops added to; & present Shoemakers Shop enlarged to 14 men, new Shops consisting of Armourers, Tailors & Smiths established.	
			Divisional Order drafted instructing all Units to send all unserviceable puttees in to Ordnance. The Tailors repair, cut off worn portions & stitch on serviceable pieces, making a great saving of material which would otherwise be burned.	
			Frogs from Band approval of issue received.	
	5 4/16		Routine. Units visited. Approval received for issue of New Wire Cutter for fixing to rifles. on scale of 64 per Infantry Battalion.	
	6 4/16		Divisional Advanced Repair Shop for Vermorel Sprayers established at Mont. St. Eloy.	
	7 4/16		Notification received that types of Grenade Carriers will shortly be available, for 150 Bucket Pattern, 150 Waistcoat pattern, & 50 Belt Bag Pattern. In addition 300 Carriers per Battalion must be made locally. These were put in hand in Divisional Tailors Shop & Units making as many as possible.	

SB

2353 Wt. W2544/1454 700,000 5/15 D. D. & L. A.D.S.S./Forms/C. 2118.

Instructions regarding War Diaries and Intelligence Summaries are contained in F. S. Regs., Part II. and the Staff Manual respectively. Title pages will be prepared in manuscript.

WAR DIARY

or

INTELLIGENCE SUMMARY.

(Erase heading not required.)

Army Form C. 2118.

Place	Date	Hour	Summary of Events and Information	Remarks and references to Appendices
	8/4/16		Routine. The allowance of 60 horse shoe nails per set of all natures, are likely to be reduced to 40 in the case of Nos 1 & 2 horse shoes, Nos. 11. 12. 13. 14 & 15 mules shoes & No. 21 pony shoes. Units notified that the greatest economy must be exercised.	
	9/4/16		Winter clothing called in :- 2nd Blanket. & Capes Macintosh. (Dismounted only) also F. S. Boots	
	10/4/16		Routine A.D.O.S. visited the Dump. Withdrawal of Winter Clothing commenced.	
	11/4/16		Routine: Units notified that demands for pullthroughs should state whether weights or cords are required only or complete.	
	12/4/16		Visited Brigade Head Quarters. everything satisfactory.	
	13/4/16		Increase of Bags tool Shoemakers authorized for 2 per Infantry & 1 per Battery. This will be of great assistance to the Divisional Units & enable men to have a chance of getting their own boots returned after repair.	
	14/4/16		The question of carrying water in the Trenches considered, Petrol cans 4 galls. suggested. Copy of Fire Orders sent to A.D.O.S.	
	15/4/16		600 Knobkerries advised from the Base.	
	16/4/16		Routine: Preparation for move to the Front Line.	
	17/4/16		Instruction received that compressed air cylinders of Strombos Horns which require recharging, should be forwarded to Heavy Mobile Workshops. Frevent.	

Instructions regarding War Diaries and Intelligence Summaries are contained in F. S. Regs., Part II. and the Staff Manual respectively. Title pages will be prepared in manuscript.

WAR DIARY
or
INTELLIGENCE SUMMARY.
(Erase heading not required.)

Army Form C. 2118.

Place	Date	Hour	Summary of Events and Information	Remarks and references to Appendices
	18 4/16		Routine	
	19 4/16		Routine.	
	20 4/16		With a view of adding more workshops to the Ordnance, names of Blacksmiths, Hammermen Shoemakers & Tailors asked for from Units	
	21 4/16		Visited 46th Divn Ordnance. Large demand for Anti Gas Goggles, owing to Lachrymatory Gas Attack	
	22 4/16		Took over 46th Divn Ordnance Store at Acq. 46th took over Ordnance 25th at Roellecourt.	
	23 4/16		Approval received for issue of Grease & Dubbin to the Trench.	
	24 4/16 25 4/16		Carried out experiments with Steel helmets, treating with khaki paint & varnish, then sprinkle sand on the wet paint, allowed to dry for 12 hours. G.O.C approved & ordered the whole Division to have all helmets done.	
	26 4/16		Routine	
	27 4/16		Shops established & in running order, of Tailors, Blacksmith, Shoemakers, & Armourers.	
	28 4/16		Routine.	
	29 4/16		Visited 3 Batteries.	
	30 4/16		Routine.	

M

2353 Wt. W2544/1454 700,000 5/15 D. D. & L. A.D.S.S./Forms/C. 2118.

25th. DIV. D. A. D. O. S.

M A Y 1 9 1 6.

VOLUME IX

Instructions regarding War Diaries and Intelligence Summaries are contained in F. S. Regs., Part II. and the Staff Manual respectively. Title pages will be prepared in manuscript.

WAR DIARY
or
INTELLIGENCE SUMMARY.
(Erase heading not required.)

of the late D.A.D.O.S. (25th Division) Capt R. Roberts

Army Form C. 2118.

MAY I JUNE

25 DADOS

Vol. 3. 4

Place	Date	Hour	Summary of Events and Information	Remarks and references to Appendices
Acq	6/5/16		Returned off leave, inspected work performed during my absence, and seen if anything of importance had occurred.	
	7/5/16.		Inspected storehouses, attended "Q" and visited A.D.O.S. 17 Corps.	
			Demanded one Q.F. 18 pounder for D111 Bde to replace one damaged by shell fire	
			Two Lewis guns received from Base for, one for 10 Cheshire, and one for 3rd Worcesters.	
			Visited Q.M 1st Wilts re issue of stores.	
	8/5/16		Visited Q branch and received various instructions.	
			Reported move of 175 Tunnelling Coy from 24 Division to 25 Division.	
			Routine	
	9/5/16		Routine visited I.O.M. Corps Workshops and ADOS 17 Corps.	
	10/5/16		One Q.F. 18 pounder received for D/111, and issued to unit.	
			Routine.	

2353 Wt. W2544/1454 700,000 5/15 D. D. & L. A.D.S.S./Forms/C. 2118.

Army Form C. 2118.

II

Instructions regarding War Diaries and Intelligence Summaries are contained in F. S. Regs., Part II. and the Staff Manual respectively. Title pages will be prepared in manuscript.

WAR DIARY
or
INTELLIGENCE SUMMARY.
(Erase heading not required.)

Place	Date	Hour	Summary of Events and Information	Remarks and references to Appendices
Acq	11/5/16		Routine, visited by A.D.O.S. 17th Corps	
	12/5/16		Routine, visited Q.M. stores 11 Lancs Fusiliers and 13 Cheshires.	
	13/5/16		Demanded one Q.F. 18 pounder gun for B/110 to replace one damaged by shellfire. Routine	
	14/5/16		Visited by D.D.O.S. 3rd Army, general routine.	
	15/5/16		Move of 1/1 Lothian and Border Horse (B Squadron) to fifth corps. Routine	
	16/5/16		One gun Q.F. 18 pdr received for B/110 Bde, and issued to unit. General routine.	
	17/5/16		General Routine.	
	18/5/16		General routine, visited A.D.O.S. 17 Corps.	
	19/5/16		Routine,	

Army Form C. 2118.

Instructions regarding War Diaries and Intelligence Summaries are contained in F. S. Regs., Part II. and the Staff Manual respectively. Title pages will be prepared in manuscript.

WAR DIARY
or
INTELLIGENCE SUMMARY.

(Erase heading not required.)

III

Place	Date	Hour	Summary of Events and Information	Remarks and references to Appendices
Acq	20/5/16		Visited I.O.M. 17 Corps, and A.D.O.S. 17 Corps. Routine.	
	21/5/16		182 Tunnelling Coy moved to 4 Corps Troops. Visited by A.D.O.S. 17 Corps. Routine.	
	22/5/16		One gun reported lost by mine explosion, belonging to 7 Bde M. G. company, arrangements made for replacement. Routine.	
	23/5/16		Demanded 18 pdr Field Carriage to replace one damaged by shell fire, belonging to A/110 Bde.	
			Two Lewis guns demanded for 11 Lancs Fusiliers to replace two reported lost in mine explosion.	
			Two Trench Mortars 2" demanded for X/25 T.M. Bty to replace two lost to enemy.	
			One Vickers M. Gun demanded for 7 Bde M. Gun Coy to replace one buried by shell fire.	
	24/5/16		Routine. Seen A.D.O.S. 17 Corps.	
	25/5/16		Two Lewis guns received for 11 Lancs Fus, issued to unit.	
			One carriage field 18 pdr received for A/110 Bde. issued to unit.	

2353 Wt. W2541/1454 700,000 5/15 D. D. & L. A.D.S.S./Forms/C. 2118.

Instructions regarding War Diaries and Intelligence Summaries are contained in F. S. Regs., Part II. and the Staff Manual respectively. Title pages will be prepared in manuscript.

WAR DIARY
or
INTELLIGENCE SUMMARY.
(Erase heading not required.)

Army Form C. 2118.

IV

Place	Date	Hour	Summary of Events and Information	Remarks and references to Appendices
	26/5/16		Two Lewis guns demanded, for 10 Cheshires, to replace lost through shellfire. Routine	
	27/5/16		Two Vickers machine gun received for 7 Bde Machine Gun Coy, issued to unit. One two inch trench mortar received for X 25 T.M. Bty issued to unit. Routine	
	28/5/16		Two Lewis guns received for 10 Cheshires, issued to unit. Demanded one Q.F. 18 pdr for B/112 brigade, to replace one condemned by I.O.M. 17 Corps. Routine	
	29/5/16		Routine, visited ADOS 17 Corps. One Q.F. 18 pdr gun received for B/112, issued to unit.	
	30/5/16		Routine, visited by A.D.O.S. and I.O.M.	
	31/5/16		General routine, visited ADOS 17 Corps; visited Roellecourt to make arrangements for Ordnance dump.	

9.8.16 R J Stanton DADOS 25th Div

2353 Wt. W2544/1454 700,000 5/15 D. D. & L. A.D.S.S./Forms/C. 2118.

25th. DIV. D. A. D. O. S.

J U N E 1 9 1 6.

VOLUME X

WAR DIARY or INTELLIGENCE SUMMARY. of the late DADOS (25th Division) Captn R. Roberts — I

(Erase heading not required.)

Army Form C. 2118.

Instructions regarding War Diaries and Intelligence Summaries are contained in F. S. Regs., Part II. and the Staff Manual respectively. Title pages will be prepared in manuscript.

Place	Date	Hour	Summary of Events and Information	Remarks and references to Appendices
Roellecourt	1/6/16		Fixed up Ordnance dump, and completed removal of stores from ACQ. Routine	
	2/6/16		Visited by ADOS 17th Corps. General Routine	
	3/6/16		Lewis machine gun demanded for 13 Cheshires to replace one buried in trenches. Routine	
	4/6/16		Visited ADOS 17 Corps, routine.	
	5/6/16		Visited 3 Worcesters, and 10 Cheshires, and found unit had not been keeping stocks in hand. 172 Tunnelling Company moved to 51st Division. Received one Lewis gun for 13 Cheshires; issued to unit. Demanded one QF. 4.5 How for D/110 Bde, one damaged by premature burst. 175 Tunnelling Coy R.E., 215 Army troops R.E, and No 7 Kite balloon section, moved to 51st Division.	
	6/6/16		Routine	
	7/6/16		Visited by ADOS 17 Corps, routine	
	8/6/16		One Q.F. 4.5" How, received and issued to D/110 Bde.	
	9/6/16		Routine.	
	10/6/16		Routine.	
	11/6/16		Routine	

2353 Wt. W2544/1454 700,000 5/15 D. D. & L. A.D.S.S./Forms/C. 2118.

Army Form C. 2118.

II

Instructions regarding War Diaries and Intelligence Summaries are contained in F. S. Regs., Part II. and the Staff Manual respectively. Title pages will be prepared in manuscript.

WAR DIARY
or
INTELLIGENCE SUMMARY.
(Erase heading not required.)

Place	Date	Hour	Summary of Events and Information	Remarks and references to Appendices
ROELLECOURT	12/6/16		Routine, visited 11 Cheshires Qr Mstr Stores, and H.Q. 75 Brigade, and C.R.A. Suspended issue of stores from base, in anticipation of move.	
	13/6/16		Visited C.R.A. routine.	
	14/6/16		Visited Frohen-le-Grand with view of making arrangements for transferring stores. Routine	
	15/6/16		Moved to FROHEN-LE-GRAND. Routine	
	16/6/16		Routine. Visited DOMART to see store for Ordnance.	
DOMART.	17/6/16		Moved to Domart. Routine	
	18/6/16		Visited by A.D.O.S. X Corps Routine.	
	19/6/16		Routine, visited A.D.O.S. X Corps, and railhead.	
	20/6/16		Routine.	
	21/6/16		Routine, visited Q.M. Stores 13 Cheshires and 11 Lancs Fusiliers.	
	22/6/16		Visited Railhead and I.O.M. X Corps. Routine.	
	23/6/16		Routine.	
	24/6/16		Visited CANAPLES, to make arrangements for Ordnance dumps.	

2353 Wt. W2544/1454 700,000 5/15 D. D. & L. A.D.S.S./Forms/C. 2118.

Instructions regarding War Diaries and Intelligence Summaries are contained in F. S. Regs., Part II. and the Staff Manual respectively. Title pages will be prepared in manuscript.

WAR DIARY
or
INTELLIGENCE SUMMARY.
(Erase heading not required.)

Army Form C. 2118.

111

Place	Date	Hour	Summary of Events and Information	Remarks and references to Appendices
CANAPLES	25/6/16		Moved to Canaples, visited by ADOS X Corps.	
	26/6/16		Routine.	
RUBEMPRÉ	27/6/16		Moved to RUBEMPRÉ, took over stores from 49 Division	
	28/6/16		Demanded one Gun Q.F. 4.5 How. to replace one handed over by D/110 Bde to 36th Divisional Artillery. Routine	
	29/6/16		Routine.	
CONTAY.	30/6/16		Moved to CONTAY. Issued one Q.F. 4.5 How, to D/110 Bde X/25 T.M. Bty. moved to 21st Division. Y/25 T.M. moved to 36th Division, Z/25 moved to 34th Division. Routine.	

R J Sturton Lt
9.8.16
DADOS 25th Division

25th. DIV. D. A. D. O. S.

J U L Y 1 9 1 6.

DAA & QMG

Attached is my diary in duplicate for July 1916. Please acknowledge receipt

R. J. Stanton Lt

1.8.16 DADOS 25 Div

VOLUME ~~III~~ 25 I — July

Army Form C. 2118.

DADOS 5

Instructions regarding War Diaries and Intelligence Summaries are contained in F. S. Regs., Part II. and the Staff Manual respectively. Title pages will be prepared in manuscript.

WAR DIARY ~~or~~ ~~INTELLIGENCE SUMMARY.~~

(Erase heading not required.)

Place	Date	~~Hour~~	Summary of Events and Information	Remarks and references to Appendices
HENNENCOURT	9/7/16		Left Bethune (33rd Division) on receiving a telegram the night before telling me to report for duty as D.A.D.O.S of the 25th Division in the place of Capt. R. Roberts killed, arrived at HENNENCOURT about 4. P.M. and reported to AA & QMG	Vol 5
"	10/7/16		Went to Railhead ACHEUX and arranged ~~[illegible]~~ to remove the dump from there to HENNENCOURT the next day, also went to CONTAY and arranged to remove the shoemakers from there to HENNENCOURT the next day. Wired to Base for 6 Lewis Machine Guns complete, lost or destroyed	
"	11/7/16		Routine work - Told by AA & QMG that Division was moving to SENLIS the next day, went over to SENLIS to make arrangements with D.A.D.O.S 32nd Division to take over Dump - Wired to Base for 13 Lewis Guns & 1 Maxim lost & destroyed	
SENLIS	12/7/16		Went with Divisional Head Quarters to SENLIS - Received 6 Lewis Guns sent for on the 10th inst. & issued same (2) to 3rd Worcester Regt (3) to 1st Wilts and (1) to 10th Cheshire Regt. Went to Railhead ACHEUX to make arrangements for delivery of these guns. Wired to Base for 6 Lewis Guns -	
	13.7.16		Received wire from Abbeville that 13 Lewis Guns and 1 Vickers (in lieu of Maxim) had been sent to Railhead ACHEUX - Went to Railhead and found the Lewis Guns & Vickers had arrived & made arrangements to send them to Units which were issued as follows:- (7) 8th Loyal N. Lancs (1) 3rd Worcesters (5) 2nd Royal Irish Rifles (1) Vickers to 7 Bde M. Gun Coy. Note 7 of the Lewis guns lost were subsequently salved & returned to Base. Wired for 2 Lewis Guns for 6th South Wales Bord[ers]	

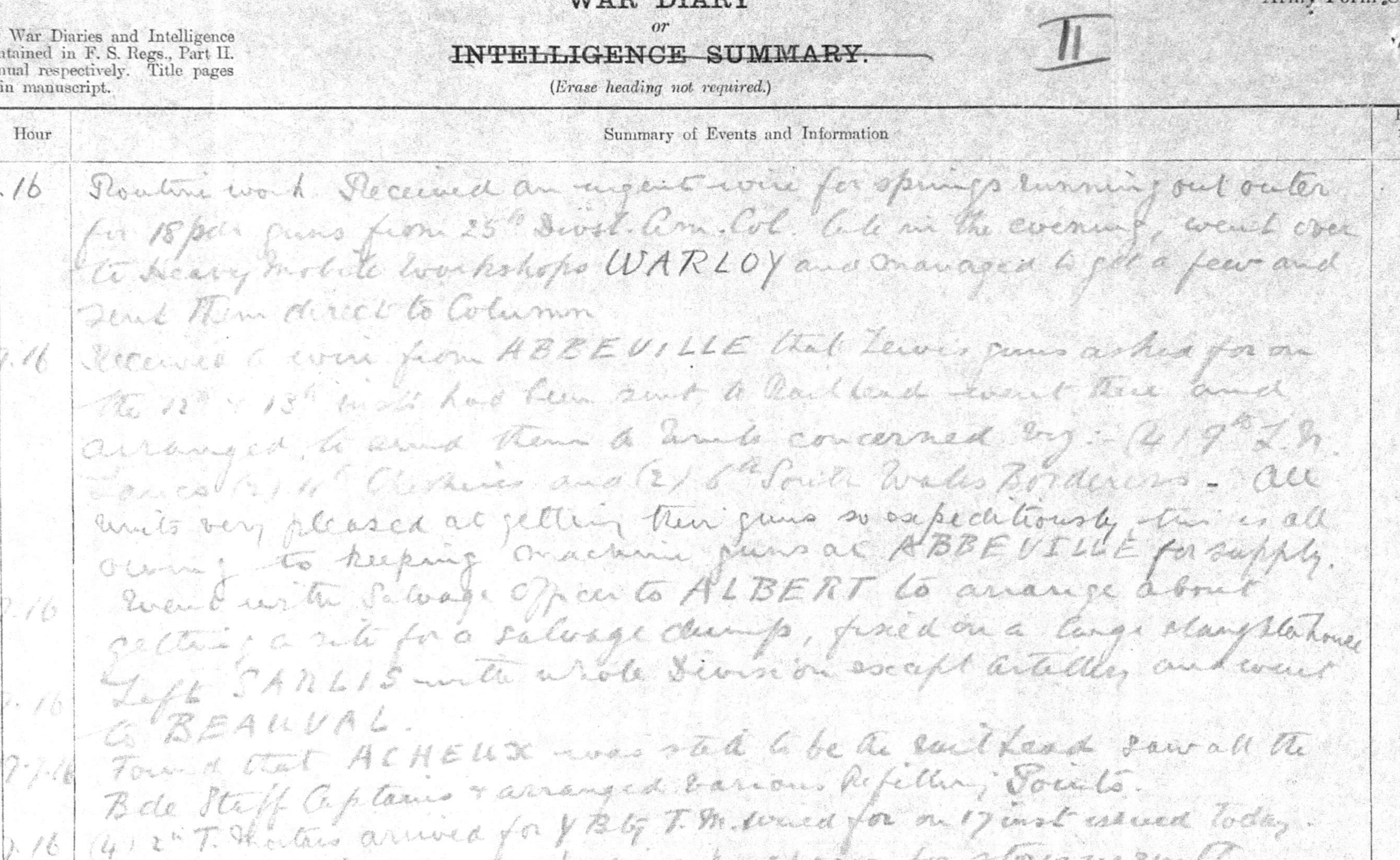

Army Form C. 2118.

WAR DIARY
or
~~INTELLIGENCE SUMMARY.~~
(Erase heading not required.)

II

Instructions regarding War Diaries and Intelligence Summaries are contained in F. S. Regs., Part II. and the Staff Manual respectively. Title pages will be prepared in manuscript.

Place	Date	Hour	Summary of Events and Information	Remarks and references to Appendices
SENLIS	14.7.16		Routine work. Received an urgent wire for springs running out outer for 18pdr guns from 25th Divsl. Am. Col. Late in the evening, went over to Heavy Mobile Workshops WARLOY and managed to get a few and sent them direct to Column	
"	15.7.16		Received a wire from ABBEVILLE that Lewis guns asked for on the 12th & 13th inst. had been sent to Railhead went there and arranged to send them to units concerned viz:- (1) 9th L.N. Lancs (2) 11th Cheshires and (2) 6th South Wales Borderers. All units very pleased at getting their guns so expeditiously - this is all owing to keeping machine guns at ABBEVILLE for supply.	
"	16.7.16		Went with Salvage Officer to ALBERT to arrange about getting a site for a salvage dump, fixed on a large slaughterhouse	
"	18.7.16		Left SANLIS with whole Division except artillery and went to BEAUVAL.	
BEAUVAL	19.7.16		Found that ACHEUX was still to be the railhead. Saw all the Bde Staff Captains & arranged various Refilling Points.	
"	20.7.16		(4) 2" T. Mortars arrived for Y Bty T.M. asked for on 17 inst. issued today. Went to AMIENS to make some purchases for stores urgently required	

Instructions regarding War Diaries and Intelligence Summaries are contained in F. S. Regs., Part II. and the Staff Manual respectively. Title pages will be prepared in manuscript.

WAR DIARY
or
INTELLIGENCE SUMMARY.
(Erase heading not required.)

Army Form C. 2118.

III

Place	Date	Hour	Summary of Events and Information	Remarks and references to Appendices
BEAUVAL	22.7.16		Move with Division from BEAUVAL to BUS.LES.ARTOIS.	
BUS	23.7.16		Went over to see A.D.O.S on various matters and went on to Railhead and arranged with Units to use old Dump at ACHEUX as Clearing Station and visit Salvage Store	
BUS	25.7.16		Move with Division from BUS to BERTRANCOURT visit dump.	
BERTRANCOURT	26.7.16		Railhead changed from ACHEUX to BELLE EGLISE. but arrange with Units to keep Clearing Station at ACHEUX.	
–	27.7.16		Visit Railhead Clearing Station and Salvage Dump.	
–	28.7.16		Visit Railhead + Clearing Station	
–	29.7.16		Meeting of Bde Staff Captains and Quarter Masters presided over by A.A.Q.M.G. Various matter discussed + outstanding questions settled. Went to see D.D.O.S Reserve Army as to the Corps the Division were going to be in and transfer of 29th Divisional artillery from 25th Div to 20th Div.	
–	30.7.16		Went to AMIENS to collect bomb carriers & washers.	
	31.7.16		Car used by D.A.D.O.S sent to Supply Col. for overhaul	

31.7.16

R. J. Sturton Lt
D.A.D.O.S
25th Div.

2353 Wt. W2544/1454 700,000 5/15 D. D. & L. A.D.S.S./Forms/C. 2118.

25th. DIV. D. A. D. O. S.

A U G U S T 1 9 1 6.

Confidential

A.A & Q.M.G.

My diary for August in duplicate herewith please

A. J. Hunter Capt

DADOS

1.9.16 25th Division

Keep all diaries together as they come in

[illegible]

Instructions regarding War Diaries and Intelligence Summaries are contained in F. S. Regs., Part II. and the Staff Manual respectively. Title Pages will be prepared in manuscript.

WAR DIARY

~~or~~

~~INTELLIGENCE SUMMARY~~

(Erase heading not required.)

Army Form C. 2118

I DADOS

Vol 6

Place	Date	~~Hour~~	Summary of Events and Information	Remarks and references to Appendices
Bertrancourt	1/8/16		Routine work.	
	2nd 3rd 4th 5th 6th		Routine work.	
	7th		Went to Railhead to see the R.T.O. and made arrangements with him to send on Steel Helmets returned by the various Salvage Officers as they were urgently required.	
	8th & 9th		Routine work	
Bus les Artois	10th		Moved with the Divisional Head Quarters from Bertrancourt to Bus les Artois, went to Doval and arranged with the O.C. Supply Column 25th Division to send him a blacksmith and his assistant and I undertook to provide the tools necessary for making stands for firing rifle smoke bombs	
	11th		Went to inspect the Dump at Canaples where the rifles with telescopic sights and other articles belonging to the units of the 25th Division had been stored during the advance & found the rifles had been withdrawn on the 25th July by units	
	12th		Routine work.	

1875 Wt. W593/826 1,000,000 4/15 J.B.C. & A. A.D.S.S./Forms/C. 2118.

25th. DIV. D. A. D. O. S.

S E P T E M B E R 1 9 1 6.

D.A.A & Q.M.G.
25th Division

Herewith my Diary for September please.

R. J. Stanton
DADOS
25th Div.

30/9/16

D.A.D.O.S. 25th Division

WAR DIARY

~~or~~

~~INTELLIGENCE SUMMARY.~~

(Erase heading not required.)

I

Army Form C. 2118.

Vol 7

Instructions regarding War Diaries and Intelligence Summaries are contained in F. S. Regs., Part II. and the Staff Manual respectively. Title pages will be prepared in manuscript.

Place	Date 1916	Hour	Summary of Events and Information	Remarks and references to Appendices
Senlis	1st Sep to 6th Sep		Routine work – On the 2nd of Sept I went home on Special leave and was relieved by Lieut J. McGowan	
Acheux	7th Sep		Divisional Head Quarters left Senlis and went to Acheux	
"	8th & 9th Sept		Routine work. On the 9th Sub Con Bracher Bde W.O. was taken ill and went to Hospital	
Doulens	10th Sep		Divisional Head Quarters moved from Acheux & went to Doulens, Returned from Leave & joined the Division	
Bernaville	11th Sep		Divisional Head Quarters moved from Doulens to Bernaville	
Domqueur Le Plouy	12th Sep		Divisional Head Quarters moved from Bernaville to Domqueur and Le Plouy. The whole of the 25th Division arrived in this area for Rest and Reequipment except the Artillery, D.A.C. & 1 Coy of A.S.C.	
"	13th, 14th, 15th 16th Sept		Routine work	
"	17th Sept		Went to Forceville to see Dump for Artillery	
"	18th " 19th " 20th "		Routine Work. Chief Clerk went on Special Leave 19th inst	

2353 Wt. W2544/1454 700,000 5/15 D. D. & L. A.D.S.S./Forms/C. 2118.

Instructions regarding War Diaries and Intelligence Summaries are contained in F. S. Regs., Part II. and the Staff Manual respectively. Title pages will be prepared in manuscript.

WAR DIARY or ~~INTELLIGENCE~~ SUMMARY. D.A.D.O.S. 25th Division. II

(*Erase heading not required.*)

Army Form C. 2118.

Place	Date 1916	Hour	Summary of Events and Information	Remarks and references to Appendices
Domqueur	21st Sept		Again visited Artillery Dump at Forceville	
"	22nd Sept		Routine work	
"	23rd "		Brigade Staff Captains & Quartermasters meeting held presided over by A.A. & Q.M.G. various questions with regard to Ordnance Supplies discussed and settled, and it was arranged that Quartermasters should make a point of attending once a month on D.A.D.O.S with all outstanding Indents with a view to Entering or cancelling them	
"	24th Sept		Routine work.	
Boval	25th Sept		Left Domqueur with Division and went to Boval	
Acheux	26th Sept		Left Boval and went to Acheux	
"	27th "		Routine work.	
"	28th "		Routine work.	
"	29th "		Routine work.	
"	30th "		Went over to Bouzincourt to see about a site for Ordnance Dump Chief Clerk returned in the evening.	

30/9/16 A. J. Sturton Lt
D.A.D.O.S 25th Division

2353 Wt. W2544/1454 700,000 5/15 D. D. & L. A.D.S.S./Forms/C. 2118.

25th. DIV. D. A. D. O. S.

O C T O B E R 1 9 1 6.

Instructions regarding War Diaries and Intelligence Summaries are contained in F. S. Regs., Part II. and the Staff Manual respectively. Title Pages will be prepared in manuscript.

WAR DIARY D.A.D.O.S 25th Division

~~or INTELLIGENCE SUMMARY~~

(Erase heading not required.)

Army Form C. 2118

I

Place	Date	Hour	Summary of Events and Information	Remarks and references to Appendices
Acheux	1/10/16		Routine work	
Henencourt	2/10/16		Division left Acheux and went to Senlis, I took over the Ordnance Dump of the 19th Division on the Senlis Henencourt Road.	
"	3/10/16		Went to inspect various places in the Bouzincourt area ~~suitable~~ for a suitable ordnance dump, but could not find one, eventually arranged with the Town Major of Bouzincourt to take a place in Bouzincourt, though out of our area, the Town Major, Major R. C. Beeson of the 8th Canadian Inf Bat was very kind in the matter and gave me the best accommodation available.	
Bouzincourt	4/10/16		Took over Dump at Bouzincourt	
"	5/10/16		Routine work	
"	6/10/16		ditto	
"	7/10/16		ditto	
"	8/10/16		Visited Salvage Dump at Aveluy to see if arrangements could be made to condition clean re the large number of rifles coming in every day from the forward area, but found the number was too great to deal with, the Divisional Head Quarters therefore obtained leave to send them direct to the Base.	

Instructions regarding War Diaries and Intelligence Summaries are contained in F. S. Regs., Part II. and the Staff Manual respectively. Title pages will be prepared in manuscript.

WAR DIARY D.A.O.S. 25th Division
~~or~~
~~INTELLIGENCE SUMMARY.~~
(Erase heading not required.)

Army Form C. 2118.

Vol 8

Place	Date	Hour	Summary of Events and Information	Remarks and references to Appendices
Bouzincourt	9/10/16		Routine work	
"	10/10/16		do	
"	11/10/16		do	
"	12/10/16		Went to Salvage Dump Aveluy and arranged to take 200 more rifles to be overhauled & cleaned by our Divisional Armourers Shop Bouzincourt.	
"	13/10/16		Routine work	
"	14/10/16		do	
"	15/10/16		do	
"	16, 17, 18/10		do	
"	19/10/16		Being warned by Divl. H.Q. that Division would be moving again, in a day or two, as several trucks of winter clothing were due to arrive the next day, went to Abbeville to see the R.O.O. Regulating Station and arranged with him to hold up trucks consigned from Acheux till notified of our new Rail head.	
"	20/10/16		Routine work	
	21/10/16		do	

2353 Wt. W2544/1454 700,000 5/15 D. D. & L. A.D.S.S./Forms/C. 2118.

Instructions regarding War Diaries and Intelligence Summaries are contained in F. S. Regs., Part II. and the Staff Manual respectively. Title pages will be prepared in manuscript.

WAR DIARY D.A.D.O.S. ~~or INTELLIGENCE SUMMARY.~~ 25th Division

(*Erase heading not required.*)

Army Form C. 2118.

III

Place	Date	Hour	Summary of Events and Information	Remarks and references to Appendices
Contay	22/10/16		Left Bouzincourt ~~[illegible]~~ and went to Contay.	
"	23/10/16		Divisional H.Q. left Bouzincourt area and went to Contay.	
~~B[illegible]~~ Beauval	24/10/16		Left Contay and went to Beauval	
	25/10/16		Routine work	
"	26/10/16		Sent to Paris by Div[l] H.Q. to arrange for the early delivery of the Divisional signs which was being made there and found that the firm making them had great difficulty in making them owing to the stamps continually breaking	
"	27/10/16		Returned from Paris and found my staff had been sent to Caestre by Div[l] H.Q. to make arrangements for receiving the stores accompanied from Abbeville	
Caestre	28/10/16		Arrived at Caestre and found my staff had arrived, but no trucks with stores or office records and furniture had come to hand.	
"	29/10/16		As no trucks had arrived got R.T.O. to wire to Calais & Abbeville to send on all trucks for 25th Division.	
"	30/10/16		No trucks arrived, but were notified by Calais & Abbeville that trucks had been despatched.	
	31/10/16		No trucks arrived.	

31/10/16 R J Sturton Capt
DADOS 25th Div

25th. DIV. D. A. D. O. S.

N O V E M B E R 1 9 1 6.

Instructions regarding War Diaries and Intelligence Summaries are contained in F. S. Regs., Part II. and the Staff Manual respectively. Title pages will be prepared in manuscript.

WAR DIARY or ~~INTELLIGENCE SUMMARY.~~ D.A.D.O.S 25th Division

(Erase heading not required.)

Army Form C. 2118.

I

Vol 13

Place	Date	Hour	Summary of Events and Information	Remarks and references to Appendices
Caestre	1/11/16		Trucks reconsigned from Somme area begin to arrive, but no trace of Truck with Office records - Received a wire from D.A.D.R.T. ABBEVILLE later in the day saying truck with office furniture and records was held there pending further instructions	
"	2/11/16		Went over to ABBEVILLE in Car to fetch most important records and gave explicit instructions for truck to be consigned to Caestre, R.C.O. in charge of Regulating Station promised it should be sent that afternoon - More trucks arrive with stores	
"	3/11/16		More trucks arrive with stores but not truck with Office records (No of truck 52015)	
"	4/11/16		Saw R.T.O. CAESTRE as to the non arrival of Truck with Office records he had no trace. Non arrival of records causing great inconvenience and some delay in issuing stores. Routine work.	
"	5/11/16		Received a wire from Ordnance 5th Army Railhead saying truck with the Office furniture and records had arrived there and had been reconsigned. This shows great carelessness on the part of the Regulating Station ABBEVILLE.	

2353 Wt. W2544/1454 700,000 5/15 D. D. & L. A.D.S.S./Forms/C. 2118.

Army Form C. 2118.

Instructions regarding War Diaries and Intelligence Summaries are contained in F. S. Regs., Part II. and the Staff Manual respectively. Title pages will be prepared in manuscript.

WAR DIARY ~~or INTELLIGENCE SUMMARY~~. DADOS 25th Division II

(Erase heading not required.)

Place	Date	Hour	Summary of Events and Information	Remarks and references to Appendices
Bailleul	6/11/16		Left CAESTRE and went to BAILLEUL took a temporary store pending the removal of the Gas school 7th Division from the store which had been allotted to DADOS in BAILLEUL. Took over Advanced Dump at DESEULE from 7th Division DADOS placed the senior Bde W.O. Mr Farrar in charge.	
"	7/11/16		Visited the new Railhead STEENWERCK and saw R.O.O and arranged about time for unloading trucks and as to drawing rifles and other stores sent to him for consignment to Base by other Divisions.	
"	8/11/16		Went to Salvage Dump at OOSTHOVE Farm nothing there of a serviceable nature. Received 9000 small box respirators	
	9th		Routine work. Arranged with the Divisional Head Quarters that the Gas Officer should receive all the Small Box Respirators at his School NIEPPE and use the empty ~~boxes~~ cases for the return to Base of the released P.H.G. P.H and Large Box Respirators.	
	10th		Received 7000 small Box Respirators and sent them to the Gas School	

Instructions regarding War Diaries and Intelligence Summaries are contained in F. S. Regs., Part II. and the Staff Manual respectively. Title pages will be prepared in manuscript.

WAR DIARY DADOS
or
~~INTELLIGENCE SUMMARY.~~ 25th Division

(*Erase heading not required.*)

Army Form C. 2118.

III

Place	Date	Hour	Summary of Events and Information	Remarks and references to Appendices
BAILLEULE	11/11/16		Routine work	
	12/11/16		Visited Salvage Dump found units had returned some Large Box Respirators contrary to orders gave strict instructions that no gas helmets of any kind were to be taken in there as units had instructions to return them to Gas Officer –	
	13th 14th 15th		Routine work	
	16th		Visited Gas Officer to see how the P.H. G. Helmets and Large Box Respirators were being returned found they were being returned very slowly arranged to wire Bde Head Quarters to hasten return	
	17th to 30th		Routine work.	

R J Hunter Capt
DADOS
25th Division
3/12/16

2353 Wt. W2544/1454 700,000 5/15 D. D. & L. A.D.S.S./Forms/C. 2118.

25th. DIV. D. A. D. O. S.

D E C E M B E R 1 9 1 6.

Headquarters G.
25th Division

Herewith War Diary
for month of December.

B. L. Humphreys Lt
a/DADOS
25th Div.

1. I. 1917

Q
Passed

Instructions regarding War Diaries and Intelligence Summaries are contained in F. S. Regs., Part II. and the Staff Manual respectively. Title pages will be prepared in manuscript.

WAR DIARY D.A.D.O.S.
or
~~INTELLIGENCE SUMMARY.~~ 25th Division

(Erase heading not required.)

Army Form C. 2118.

Vol I 70

Place	Date	~~Hour~~	Summary of Events and Information	Remarks and references to Appendices
Bailleul	1/12/16		attending at Gas Officer's School Nieppe to see how he was getting on with the fitting of Units with Small Box Respirators found they were not returning P.H.G. Helmets in the numbers expected. also visited Salvage Officer about a new dump for	
	2/12/16		Wrote Units urging return of P.H.G helmets as they were badly wanted at base.	
	3rd 4th 5th		Routine work & visiting Q.Ms Stores	
	6th		New huts for 7th & 74th Bdes being finished arranged to take over old hut for Shoemakers and Armourers workshops.	
	7th 8th 9th		Routine work & visiting Q.Ms Stores, found that in several cases, body ~~belts~~ bands had not been issued the reason given was the difficulty of getting them washed in consequence arranged with Div. H.Q. that some should be kept at the Divl Baths for exchange	

Instructions regarding War Diaries and Intelligence Summaries are contained in F. S. Regs., Part II. and the Staff Manual respectively. Title pages will be prepared in manuscript.

WAR DIARY D.A.D.O.S
or
~~INTELLIGENCE SUMMARY.~~ 25th Div.

(*Erase heading not required.*)

Army Form C. 2118.

II

Place	Date	Hour	Summary of Events and Information	Remarks and references to Appendices
		1916		
BAILLEUL	10th	Dec	Visiting Gas Officer to urge completion of Artillery Units with Small Box Respirators & return of P.H.G. Helmets, went to see C.R.A. on that subject and as to return of surplus stores on reorganization of Artillery into 6 gun batteries arranging for a store for the surplus articles to be returned after being cleaned & labelled	
	11th 12th		Routine work & visiting QM's Stores.	
	13th		Visiting C.R.A. on various matters connected with Trench Mortars & Trench Mortar Hand Carts & arranging to lend him my Sergt Clerk to superintend the packing of surplus stores released on reorganization of artillery	
	14th		Went to Calais Ordnance Depot with a list of outstanding Indents to see if there was a chance of them being supplied at an early date found that very few of the articles were available – The A.D.O.S IX Corps also went with me as he wished to see the Salvage Stores and Workshops.	

Instructions regarding War Diaries and Intelligence Summaries are contained in F. S. Regs., Part II. and the Staff Manual respectively. Title pages will be prepared in manuscript.

WAR DIARY ~~or INTELLIGENCE SUMMARY.~~ D.A.D.O.S 25th Division III

(Erase heading not required.)

Army Form C. 2118.

Place	Date 1916	Hour	Summary of Events and Information	Remarks and references to Appendices
BAILLEUL	15 Dec		My motor car driver reported that the car was showing serious defects in two or three places, went with him to the II Australian Supply Column, the O.C said he thought car was beyond local repair & he would report same to D.T.S & T with a view to its being sent to Base to be replaced by another car.	
"	16 Dec		Having received a heavy demand for harness from No 4 Sec D.A.C went over to see the Q.M. inspected harness & found a good deal was beyond local repair and was getting dangerous & should be replaced & arranging accordingly.	
"	17th "		Routine work, found very inconvenient not having a car for visiting forward dump, salvage &c. The Supply Column had not yet received a reply from D.T.S & T	
"	18th "			
"	19th "		Borrowed one of Q. cars went to D.A.D.O.S 16 Div. for 25 Canadian Packs found only 10 had been used by him for one, went on to No 1 & 2 Secs DAC to inspect their [illegible] & to know why so many surcingles had been demanded, the O.C. claimed he was entitled to surcingles for every animal in order to secure the blanket on the animal, arranged to raise the point with ADOS IX Corps	

2353 Wt. W2544/1454 700,000 5/15 D. D. & L. A.D.S.S./Forms/C. 2118.

Instructions regarding War Diaries and Intelligence Summaries are contained in F. S. Regs., Part II. and the Staff Manual respectively. Title pages will be prepared in manuscript.

WAR DIARY D.A.D.O.S
or
~~INTELLIGENCE SUMMARY.~~
(Erase heading not required.)

25th Division IV

Army Form C. 2118.

Place	Date 1916	Hour	Summary of Events and Information	Remarks and references to Appendices
BAILLEUL	20th Dec		Arranging for the erection of a "Williams" Hut for the accommodation of the [illegible] W.Os as I intended to move dump from Bailleul to de Seule Forward Dump. Visit Salvage Officer & found he had a spare Armstrong Hut which he had salved, arranged with H.Q. that this could be handed over for use at de Seule dump (Still without a car)	
"	21st "		Routine work	
"	22nd "		More Bailleul dump down to de Seule forward dump	
"	23rd "		Routine work and making arrangements for Christmas day	
"	24th "		Visited 74th Machine Gun Coy as they had put in a request for an old G.S. wagon wheel for a mounting for a machine gun against aircraft, arranging that they could draw a condemned wheel from Salvage for experimental purposes. Also visited No 2 Sec D.A.C. informed O.C. that the surcingles demanded by them for the off animal could not be obtained as it was no longer required as the off animal was no longer used as a saddle animal.	

2353 Wt. W2544/1454 700,000 5/15 D. D. & L. A.D.S.S./Forms/C. 2118.

Instructions regarding War Diaries and Intelligence Summaries are contained in F. S. Regs., Part II. and the Staff Manual respectively. Title pages will be prepared in manuscript.

WAR DIARY

or

~~INTELLIGENCE SUMMARY.~~

(Erase heading not required.)

Army Form C. 2118.

DADOS 25th D.W. V

Place	Date	Hour	Summary of Events and Information	Remarks and references to Appendices
Bailleul	25th Dec		Routine work	
	26th	-	Routine work. Visited advanced Dumps at De Seule	
	27th	-	Routine work. Capt. Sturton left Bailleul 3pm for England. ADOS tried on 10 days leave. Lieut B. J. Humphrys ADO Takes over duties. 3 men for mines.	
	28	-	Purchased material for Flags for G. Branch. Attended Staff Captains conference at Pont de Nieppe. Moved Office from Bailleul to De Seule	
	29	-	Visited by ADOS. 9th Corps. Fatigues cleared refuse from Dumps.	
	30	-	Purchased remainder of material for Flags. Routine work.	
	31	-	Sent lorry to 2nd Pontoon Park for Pit props also to H.Q. D.W. to deliver Flags. Routine work. Fatigue party of 2 NCOs + 12 men dug drainage trenches round huts.	

B J Humphrys Lt
DADOS
25th Div

1.I.1917

2353 Wt. W2544/1454 700,000 5/15 D. D. & L. A.D.S.S./Forms/C. 2118.

Confidential 25/S/179

D.A.D.O.S.

25th Division

Enclosed please find a my War Diary for the month of January.

R J Sturton
Capt
D.A.D.O.S.
25th Div

2/2/17

Instructions regarding War Diaries and Intelligence Summaries are contained in F. S. Regs., Part II. and the Staff Manual respectively. Title pages will be prepared in manuscript.

WAR DIARY
or
~~INTELLIGENCE SUMMARY.~~

(Erase heading not required.)

DADOS 25th Div

Vol ~~XI~~ I

Army Form C. 2118.

Place	Date 1917	Hour	Summary of Events and Information	Remarks and references to Appendices
Jan Le Sentier	1		Visited by AAQMG & DAQMG. Sent lorry to 2nd Pontoon Park to fetch Pit Props. Forwarded remainder of Flags to DHQ. Q am.	
–	2		Visited by ADOS 9th Corps. Repairs to Cookhouse carried out. " " OC. 106th Fd Co REs re work to be carried out at Dump	
	3		Routine work. Visited Divl. Salvage officer. Repairs to dump walls.	
	4 5 6 7		Routine work.	
	8		Return from 10 days leave & take over from Lieut Humphreys	
	9		Routine work	
	10th		Visit No 1 Sec D.A.C. to inspect harness find that 13 Saddles required new rear arches arrange to have these sent to the Base & to be replaced.	
	11		Visit Salvage & other units & point out the necessity of greater care being exercised in submitting indents for clothing boots & necessaries & that only articles required for immediate issue should be demanded & that the greatest economy should be practised.	

2353 Wt. W2544/1454 700,000 5/15 D. D. & L. A.D.S.S./Forms/C. 2118.

Instructions regarding War Diaries and Intelligence Summaries are contained in F. S. Regs., Part II. and the Staff Manual respectively. Title pages will be prepared in manuscript.

WAR DIARY
or
~~INTELLIGENCE SUMMARY.~~
(Erase heading not required.)

Army Form C. 2118.

DA.D.O.S
25th Division
II

Place	Date	Hour	Summary of Events and Information	Remarks and references to Appendices
	1917			
St Sevle	12		Visiting Q. M. Stores of two units pointing out to the Q. Masters the necessity of keeping a very strict watch on the issue of clothing boots & necessaries & that they should personally satisfy themselves that clothing was quite unserviceable before replacing it.	
	13		Routine work. Having received a very heavy Indent for clothing visited the Quarter Master of the 76th Field Ambulance who was new to his job pointing out that only articles required for immediate issue were to be demanded & that he should hold nothing in reserve he arranged to cut down his Indent accordingly	
	14.		Routine work visit Salvage. no stores in hand which I required	
	15		Visit several units with regard to Indents for clothing point out that their demands appear excessive especially having regard to the issues to them for the last quarter even taking into consideration the requipment necessary after leaving the Somme. I saw the O.C. of one unit where demand was heavy & explaining that I quite understood his desire to see his unit smart & well dressed, but that owing to the enormous amount of clothing required for the Armies in the Field & at home the expense to the	

Instructions regarding War Diaries and Intelligence Summaries are contained in F. S. Regs., Part II. and the Staff Manual respectively. Title pages will be prepared in manuscript.

WAR DIARY

~~or~~

~~INTELLIGENCE SUMMARY.~~

(Erase heading not required.)

D.A.D.O.S 25th Division

Army Form C. 2118.

111

Place	Date	Hour	Summary of Events and Information	Remarks and references to Appendices
~~Bailleul~~ De Seule	1917 15		(con) country was very great and that service dress could only be replaced on becoming quite unserviceable, the O.C. quite saw the necessity for economy and promised that demands for replacement should only be submitted when the necessity clearly arose.	
"	16		Went to Dunkirk with the DADOS of 36th Div to try & purchase French road brooms & refills for electric torches but after trying several shops & making enquiries found these brooms were not obtainable and that the refills were too expensive –	
"	17		Owing to the heavy demands for service dress & boots by the Pioneer Bat. to which I had raised objection & which the O.C. of the Bat. put down to the conditions under which they had to work & the distance they had to march to the trenches every day, went round the trenches with him & saw some of the working parties	
"	18		Routine work	
	19		Having received some rather excessive Indents from two of the Sections of the D.A.C. for Pantaloons & Service Caps and	

2353 Wt. W2544/1454 700,000 5/15 D. D. & L. A.D.S.S./Forms/C. 2118.

Instructions regarding War Diaries and Intelligence Summaries are contained in F. S. Regs., Part II. and the Staff Manual respectively. Title pages will be prepared in manuscript.

WAR DIARY or ~~INTELLIGENCE SUMMARY.~~

(Erase heading not required.)

D.A.D.O.S. 25th Division

Army Form C. 2118.

IV

Place	Date	Hour	Summary of Events and Information	Remarks and references to Appendices
Le Seule	19 (con)		necessaries visiting the O.C.s with a view to ascertain the reasons for such demands ascertaining that the pantaloons now being supplied were of inferior quality & soon wore out and that the caps soon lost their shape and complaints had been made as to the untidy appearance of the men by inspecting officers, but that they were not unserviceable, also interviewing the O.C. H.Q. Sn. D.A.C. on the subject & arranging to write to him with particulars, writing accordingly.	
"	20		Routine work	
"	21		do	
"	22		I received a letter from the O.C. Hd Qrs D.A.C. in reply to mine of the 19th inst stating that Razors & other necessaries if lost by the men by neglect were being charged against them, but that the razors were made of very poor metal & did not last long and that there was no doubt the demands were excessive, which could be partly accounted for by the reasons given & that he would again warn the O.C. Sections as to the necessity of strict supervision & economy. He also suggested in his letter that if pantaloons were made of the old fashioned corduroy they would last 10 times as long as the present ones, in consequence of this suggestion seeing the A.D.O.S. IX Corps, but he was of the opinion that it would be impossible to get a sufficient quantity of the material & it would also be too expensive	

Instructions regarding War Diaries and Intelligence Summaries are contained in F. S. Regs., Part II. and the Staff Manual respectively. Title pages will be prepared in manuscript.

WAR DIARY ~~or INTELLIGENCE SUMMARY.~~ D.A.D.O.S. 25th Division

(*Erase heading not required.*)

Army Form C. 2118.

V

Place	Date	Hour	Summary of Events and Information	Remarks and references to Appendices
De Seule	23		Chief Clerk went on leave, Routine work	
	24		Routine work. Having received an Indent for two 2" Trench Mortars for Y/25 T.M.B. certified as being destroyed by shell fire by D.T.M.O. wiring for same, but on asking for the numbers of the guns destroyed from the C.R.A. I ascertained incidentally that the guns had apparently not been destroyed but had been sent to the I.O.M. I therefore telephoned to the I.O.M. & he informed me that he had received the two T. Mortars & that he thought they could be repaired in the Shops, cancelling the Indent accordingly & reporting the matter to Div. H.Q. & C.R.A.	
	25		Routine work	
	26		On visiting the wagon lines of No 4 Sec D.A.C a short time ago the O.C. drew my attention to some wagons ammunition 15 Pdr which had been left behind by the 7th D.A.C & I then arranged that he should report the matter to me officially, having received a report from him that there were 10 wagons, arranging with Railhead for their return to the Base & reporting the matter to the A.D.O.S. XV Corps	
	27		Routine work	
	28		do	

2353 Wt. W2544/1454 700,000 5/15 D. D. & L. A.D.S.S./Forms/C. 2118.

Instructions regarding War Diaries and Intelligence Summaries are contained in F. S. Regs., Part II. and the Staff Manual respectively. Title pages will be prepared in manuscript.

WAR DIARY
or
~~INTELLIGENCE SUMMARY.~~

(Erase heading not required.)

D.A.D.O.S. 25th Division

Army Form C. 2118.

VI

Place	Date	Hour	Summary of Events and Information	Remarks and references to Appendices
De Seule	29		Having received a wire from D.O.M. IX Corps condemning an 18 Pdr gun and carriage belonging to B/112 Bde R.F.A. wired for same accordingly.	
do	30		Visiting the O.C. 195th Machine Gun Coy, as one of his men, who had been pulled up by the A.P.M. for being without horse rugs for his mules, had reported that the Coy had none. ~~The~~ O.C. informed me that he had his full complement. Informing Divisional H.Q. accordingly.	
do	31		Routine work. –	

R. J. Stanton Capt
D.A.D.O.S.
25th Division

2/2/17

Instructions regarding War Diaries and Intelligence Summaries are contained in F. S. Regs., Part II. and the Staff Manual respectively. Title pages will be prepared in manuscript.

WAR DIARY D.A.D.O.S

or

~~INTELLIGENCE SUMMARY.~~ 25th Division

(Erase heading not required.)

Army Form C. 2118.

Vol I/7

Place	Date	Hour	Summary of Events and Information	Remarks and references to Appendices
De Seule	1.2.17		Attending at the C.R.A. 25th Division with reference to the reorganisation of the 113 Bde confirming that C 113 had been broken up and absorbed by D110 and D112 making them 6 gun batteries	
De Seule	2.2.17		Attending at Salvage and inspecting the new Salvage dumps and impressing on O.C. Salvage the necessity of very carefully scrutinizing all clothing returned by units to make sure it was quite unserviceable before accepting it	
"	3.2.17		Attending at 75th Bde H.Q. with reference to various outstanding Indents and as to obtaining various articles for a raid	
"	4.2.17		Visiting Divl Baths to know the position with regard to socks shirts and drawers, found that there was a large accumulation of clothing to be washed owing to a shortage of coal, arranging ~~[illegible]~~ for a special issue of 1000 socks for the 8th South Wales Bdrs who required them very urgently	
"	5.2.17		Routine work	
"	6.2.17		Attending a conference of D.O.Os at the A.D.O.S IX Corps discussing various matters and obtaining his authority to draw some white calico for making overalls for raiding parties in the snow, sending same to Divl Baths Nieppe to be made up by the women employed there	

2353 Wt. W2544/1454 700,000 5/15 D. D. & L. A.D.S.S./Forms/C. 2118.

Instructions regarding War Diaries and Intelligence Summaries are contained in F. S. Regs., Part II. and the Staff Manual respectively. Title pages will be prepared in manuscript.

WAR DIARY ~~or INTELLIGENCE SUMMARY.~~ D.A.D.O.S 25th Division

(Erase heading not required.)

Army Form C. 2118.

II

Place	Date	Hour	Summary of Events and Information	Remarks and references to Appendices
AcSeule	7.2.17		Having received an urgent message from D.T.M.O. for Lee Enfield Mechanisms for firing 2" Trench Mortars attending at IX Corps Workshops found that they had none available at the moment but were making them arranging to send 2 Armourer S. Sgts to help	
"	8.2.17		Attending at IX Corps Workshops drawing 3 Lee Enfield Mechanisms taking same to D.T.M.O. & found that all T. Mortars would then be in action. Attending at 75 Bde H.Q. with a rifle to which a electric torch had been affixed with wire attachment to be used by raiding parties for their approval.	
"	9.2.17		Attending in various Units with regard to outstanding Indents	
"	10.2.17		The H.Q. 75th Bde having returned rifle with electric torch attachment with a very favourable report and asking for 14 more to fixed up purchasing 14 electric torches and instructing armourers to affix same to rifles	
"	11.2.17		Attending at No 4 Sec D.A.C. with an Indent for Lamps Hurricane in lieu of Lamps G.S. ascertaining that they could carry on without them for a short time as G.S. Lamps would be available shortly.	
"	12.2.17		Attending at 75th Bde H.Q with regard to various matters in connection with a raid also visiting Div. Baths and Salvage Dump.	
"	13.2.17		Having received several Lee Enfield Mechanisms from D.T.M.O unserviceable with an urgent demand for replacement, attending at IX Corps Workshops drawing some and taking same to D.T.M.O.	

2353 Wt. W2544/1454 700,000 5/15 D. D. & L. A.D.S.S./Forms/C. 2118.

Instructions regarding War Diaries and Intelligence Summaries are contained in F. S. Regs., Part II. and the Staff Manual respectively. Title pages will be prepared in manuscript.

WAR DIARY ~~or INTELLIGENCE SUMMARY.~~ D.A.D.O.S 25th Division

(Erase heading not required.)

Army Form C. 2118.

III

Place	Date	Hour	Summary of Events and Information	Remarks and references to Appendices
De Seule	14.2.17		Routine work.	
"	15.2.17		Having received an urgent message that 4 2" T. Mortars were out of action for want of Lee Enfield Mechanisms again attending at IX Corps Workshops drawing 4 mechanisms and attending with same at D.T.M.O	
"	16.2.17		Incase of another urgent demand from D.T.M.O for Lee Enfield Mechanisms attending at IX Corps Workshops drawing 3 more also attending at C.R.A. reporting these continual demands arranging to wire to Base to hasten outstanding Indent for same.	
"	17.2.17		Visiting 3rd Worcesters and 8 Lyl North Lancs with reference to heavy demands for clothing enquiring into the reason for such demands when it was arranged that the demands should be reconsidered	
"	18.2.17		Attending at 75th Bde H.Q with wicks for a raid also attending at Salvage Dump and D.T.M.O with some more Lee Enfield Mechanisms and ascertaining that he had now 2 in reserve.	
"	~~18.2.17~~		Proceeding to Caestre to make arrangements for an Ordnance Dump workshops and Offices	
"	19.2.17		Routine work.	

2353 Wt. W2544/1454 700,000 5/15 D. D. & L. A.D.S.S./Forms/C. 2118.

Instructions regarding War Diaries and Intelligence Summaries are contained in F. S. Regs., Part II. and the Staff Manual respectively. Title pages will be prepared in manuscript.

WAR DIARY ~~or INTELLIGENCE SUMMARY.~~ D.A.D.O.S 25th Division

(Erase heading not required.)

Army Form C. 2118.

IV

Place	Date	Hour	Summary of Events and Information	Remarks and references to Appendices
A Senlis	20.2.17		Proceeding to St. Omer calling on A.O. Clothing Depot ascertaining that St Omer was the railhead for Tatinghem and district then proceeding to Tatinghem attending on the Mayor and arranging for a building for an Ordnance Dump there for supplying the 74th Bde and Divisional Artillery	
"	21.2.17		Routine work	
"	22.2.17		Sending Sgt Clerk (Sgt Durrant) with two lorries and four men to TATINGHEM to open Dump there. Routine work	
"	23.2.17		Routine work & making arrangements at Caestre for opening dump and workshops on the following day	
"	24.2.17		Sending stores workshops and Bde. Ro. O.S and men to Caestre in the afternoon	
Caestre	25.2.17		Moving with office to Caestre and attending at Tatinghem at the Dump ascertaining things were running well & all units had drawn their stores bringing back Indents & other papers.	
"	26.2.17		Routine work	
"	27.2.17		Attending at TATINGHEM Dump & making arrangements as to a special issue of boots to Units of 74th Bde owing to non arrival of leather from the Base	
"	28.2.17		Capt J.S. Stewart-Wallace arrives from England and reports for duty with a view to shortly taking over the appointment of D.A.D.O.S. to the 25th Division	

1/3/17 A.J. Stinton Capt.
D.A.D.O.S. 25th Division

2353 Wt. W2544/1454 700,000 5/15 D. D. & L. A.D.S.S./Forms/C. 2118.

Instructions regarding War Diaries and Intelligence Summaries are contained in F. S. Regs., Part II. and the Staff Manual respectively. Title pages will be prepared in manuscript.

WAR DIARY D.A.D.O.S 25th Division
or
~~INTELLIGENCE SUMMARY.~~
(Erase heading not required.)

Army Form C. 2118.

Vol I/16

Place	Date	Hour	Summary of Events and Information	Remarks and references to Appendices
Caestre	1.3.17		Routine work and attending at Ordnance Dump TATINGHEM on various matters	
"	2.3.17		Attending at the D.D.O.S 2nd Army arranging for the hastening of the 11 G.S. Limbered wagons for the carriage of the Lewis Machine Guns also informing him that leather sole bends were urgently required as none had been received from the Base for 2 weeks. the D.D.O.S arranged that the 25th Division should have priority in supply. Then proceeding to the Ordnance Dump TATINGHEM arranging for a special issue of boots to the 2nd R. Irish Rifles as leather for repair of boots was not available.	
	3.3.17		Routine work	
	4.3.17		Routine work and attending at the Ordnance Dump TATINGHEM with detail stores for the Artillery and arranging to send another Lorry as the N.C.O in charge there found that some of the Units in that area were too far away to come in draw stores every day	
	5.3.17		Routine work	
	6.3.17		Routine work and attending at Ordnance Dump TATINGHEM with detail stores for the Artillery and 74th Bde and ascertaining that there was a good stock of boots for immediate issue which was necessary owing to the non arrival of leather from the Base	

2353 Wt. W2544/1454 700,000 5/15 D. D. & L. A.D.S.S./Forms/C. 2118.

Instructions regarding War Diaries and Intelligence Summaries are contained in F. S. Regs., Part II. and the Staff Manual respectively. Title pages will be prepared in manuscript.

WAR DIARY

~~INTELLIGENCE SUMMARY~~.

(Erase heading not required.)

D.A.D.O.S
25th Division II

Army Form C. 2118.

Place	Date	~~Hour~~	Summary of Events and Information	Remarks and references to Appendices
Caestre	7.3.17		Routine work, arranging with the D.A.D.O.S. 36th Division to send stores for the X. Y. Z and W. Trench Mortar Batteries to him for distribution as these batteries were still in the line	
"	8.3.17		Attending with detail stores for the X. Y. Z and W. Trench Mortar Batteries at 36th Divisional Ordnance Dump DU SEULE also attending at the D.D.O.S 2nd Army H.Q. informing him that no leather had yet arrived, also that the 11 G.S. Limbered Wagons complete turn outs for the carriage of Lewis machine guns had not yet been notified as being sent, he arranged to telephone to the Base about these matters. Also proceeding to HAZEBROUCK to make various local purchases	
"	9.3.17		Attending at Ordnance Dump TATINGHEM finding that leather for boots had at last arrived also ascertaining that there were plenty of boots left out of the 600 extra pairs sent there for emergency purposes, instructing N.C.O. in charge that he was to give boots to all units who urgently required them. Also attending at H.Q. 2nd R. Irish Rifles TATINGHEM under instructions from A.D.O.S IX Corps [illegible] which he wanted me to condemn as it was too far to send to I.O.M. condemning it accordingly.	

2351 Wt. W2544/1454 700,000 5/15 D. D. & L. A.D.S.S./Forms/C. 2118.

Instructions regarding War Diaries and Intelligence Summaries are contained in F. S. Regs., Part II. and the Staff Manual respectively. Title pages will be prepared in manuscript.

WAR DIARY D.A.D.O.S.
or
~~INTELLIGENCE SUMMARY.~~ 25th Division

(Erase heading not required.)

Army Form C. 2118.

III

Place	Date	~~Hour~~	Summary of Events and Information	Remarks and references to Appendices
Caestre	10.3.17		Routine work, attending at Railhead St Omer seeing the	
	11.3.17		D.A.D.R.T. to know whether it could be arranged that the whole of the 25th Division could be supplied from St Omer Railhead he could then give me no information, then proceeding to TATINGHEM ordnance Dump on various matters. Proceeding in the afternoon to HAZEBROUCK purchasing material for armbands for runners for the 3 Brigades of Infantry.	
	12.3.17		Proceeding to St Martin and arranging for a Dump there for the 74th & 75 Bdes and all artillery units also proceeding to TATINGHEM making arrangements with the N.C.O in charge of Ordnance Dump to transfer all stores to the new Dump at St MARTIN tomorrow. Capt J. S. Stewart-Wallace attending at a Farm near EBBLINGHEM and arranging to open an Ordnance Dump there for the 7th Inf. Bde.	
	13.3.17		Handing over Imprest account, cash, secret codes and other documents to Capt J. S. Stewart-Wallace on his taking over the appointment of D.A.D.O.S. 25th Division.	

2353 Wt. W2544/1454 700,000 5/15 D. D. & L. A.D.S.S./Forms/C. 2118.

Instructions regarding War Diaries and Intelligence Summaries are contained in F. S. Regs., Part II. and the Staff Manual respectively. Title pages will be prepared in manuscript.

WAR DIARY or INTELLIGENCE SUMMARY. D.A.D.O.S.

(Erase heading not required.)

25 Division

Army Form C. 2118.

Place	Date	~~Hour~~	Summary of Events and Information	Remarks and references to Appendices
Caestre	13/3/17		Immediately after taking over from Captain Sturton A.O.D. on his giving up position of D.A.D.O.S. of the 25th Division proceeded to remove Office + Dump to St Martin (St MARTIN) and open a 2nd Dump near EBBLINGHAM.	
	14/3/17		Proceeded to CALAIS to consult C.O.O. regarding Indents etc	
	15/3/17		Proceeded from St MARTIN to Ordnance Dump EBBLINGHAM on various matters.	
	16/3/17		Routine Work.	
	17/3/17		Proceeded ordnance Dump EBBLINGHAM on various matters.	
	18/3/17.		Routine work. A.D.O.S. IX Corps inspected Dump at St Martin and found everything satisfactory.	
	19/3/17		Proceeded Merris and NEUF BERQUIN to select site for new Ordnance Dumps, Offices + Billets.	

2353 Wt. W2544/1454 700,000 5/15 D. D. & L. A.D.S.S./Forms/C. 2118.

Instructions regarding War Diaries and Intelligence Summaries are contained in F. S. Regs., Part II. and the Staff Manual respectively. Title pages will be prepared in manuscript.

WAR DIARY *or* INTELLIGENCE SUMMARY. D.A.D.O.S. 25th Division

(*Erase heading not required.*)

Army Form C. 2118.

Place	Date	Hour	Summary of Events and Information	Remarks and references to Appendices
Merris	20/3/17		On the Division moving proceeded to move Ordnance Offices and Dumps from St. MARTIN au Laert to MERRIS also opened a Dump at NEUF BERQUIN for the Artillery Units.	
	21/3/17		Proceeded to Bailleul to report to A.D.O.S. II A & N.Z.A.C. Corps on being placed in that Corps. Then proceeded to O.O. Corps Troops at Croix du Bac to obtain an Oil Heating Stove for "G" Branch Head Quarters 25th Division	
	22/3/17		Proceeded to Ordnance Dump at NEUF BERQUIN and found everything in order. Proceeded to SWARTENBROUCK where the 6th South Wales Borderers were billeted to deliver some special Stores to the C.O. & while there inspected the Q.M. Stores with him and found everything in order. The C.O. was quite satisfied with the manner in which ordnance Services were being carried out.	
	23/3/17.		A.D.O.S. II Anzac inspected Office and Ordnance Dump at MERRIS. I Showed him some returns I had prepared as to the quantity of S.D. Clothing and Boots which had been issued during 1916 and he expressed himself as satisfied.	

2353 Wt. W2544/1454 700,000 5/15 D. D. & L. A.D.S.S./Forms/C. 2118.

Instructions regarding War Diaries and Intelligence Summaries are contained in F. S. Regs., Part II. and the Staff Manual respectively. Title pages will be prepared in manuscript.

WAR DIARY *or* INTELLIGENCE SUMMARY. DADOS 25 Division

(Erase heading not required.)

Army Form C. 2118.

Place	Date	Hour	Summary of Events and Information	Remarks and references to Appendices
Merris	24:3:17		Proceeded to STEENWERCK and interviewed area Officer as to the possibility of obtaining an ordnance dump in his area. Such Barns as he showed me were wholly unsuitable being much too small and with roofs leaking very badly. I then went with him to CROIX DU BEC to inspect some possible huts. The position was not very suitable nor is the accomodation what is required, but I arranged that if nothing better could be done that I would fall back on it. I then proceeded to the Town Major at Bailleul as to the possibility of accomodation in Bailleul. In his absence I was informed by his Interpreter + S. Sergeant that no place whatever there. I reported this to A A + Q.M.G. + A.D.O.S. II Anzac.	
	25:3:17		Being informed by A.A+Q.M.G. that the IX Corps had secured a store at BAILLEUL I proceeded to Town Major of BAILLEUL and took the store he suggested. I then proceeded to DE SEULE and saw the A.A.Q.M.G. of the New Zealand Division with a view to securing a store at DE SEULE. I then proceeded to interview the Staff Captain of the 74 Bde and saw the Q.Ms of the 9th L.N. Lancs Regt. and 13th Cheshires. I also inspected their Stores and cautioned them about holding reserves and the growing need for economy. I then went to ARMENTIAIRE and visited the 11th Lancs. Fusiliers and saw the C.O.	

2353 Wt. W2541/1454 700,000 5/15 D. D. & L. A.D.S.S./Forms/C. 2118.

Instructions regarding War Diaries and Intelligence Summaries are contained in F. S. Regs., Part II. and the Staff Manual respectively. Title pages will be prepared in manuscript.

WAR DIARY
or
INTELLIGENCE SUMMARY.
(Erase heading not required.)

Army Form C. 2118.

Place	Date	Hour	Summary of Events and Information	Remarks and references to Appendices
Merris	26/3/17.		Proceeded to BAILLEUL to obtain key of Stores as arranged with A. A. Q. M. G. 25 Division on arrival found that there was considerable misunderstand, that the 36th Division were in possession and had no instructions to hand over the key. I saw Town Major and proceeded to "Q" IX Corp. After very considerable delay I obtained authority to obtain the key. On proceeding to the Store 1 Rue de Poissons I found it party filled with straw and wholly inadequate for our purposes. I at once proceeded to DE SEULE and arranged with the New Zealand Division to obtain a store there. I took an Office for my own use at BAILLEUL. In the afternoon the A.A + Q. M. G. gave me urgent instructions to obtain 2000 empty petrol tins by 9.00 a.m. on the 29th inst. I proceeded to Caestre Railhead and saw the R. S. O. + arranged with him to obtain all the returned tins. I also arranged with the R. S. O. STEENWERCKE to obtain all the tins returned to that Railhead. Returned to Merris and shifted my Office to BAILLEUL and Ordnance Dump to Store in BAILLEUL and at DE SEULE.	
BAILLEUL	27/3/17		Routine work.	

2353 Wt. W2544/1454 700,000 5/15 D. D. & L. A.D.S.S./Forms/C. 2118.

Instructions regarding War Diaries and Intelligence Summaries are contained in F. S. Regs., Part II. and the Staff Manual respectively. Title pages will be prepared in manuscript.

WAR DIARY
or
INTELLIGENCE SUMMARY.
(Erase heading not required.)

Army Form C. 2118.

Place	Date	Hour	Summary of Events and Information	Remarks and references to Appendices
Bailleul	28/3/17.		Proceeded to visit Ordnance Dump DE SEULE to enquire regarding a complaint made to Army Commander by the O.C. 8th North Lancs. as to a shortage of BOOTS. On enquiry I found that all indented for had been issued except 3 pairs. Routine. About 5.0c I received notice through "Q" that I must immediately vacate the Dump at DE SEULE. I at once proceeded there to make arrangements and secured permission through "Q" to move the Dump to 190 Rue de la Gare Bailleul.	
	29/3/17.		Made arrangements to move my Office to 167 Rue de la Gare and attended a Conference at the Office of the A.D.O.S. II Anzac. Proceeded to St. Omer under instructions of D.D.O.S. L of C North to interview him. He informed that he wished to have a personal interview with me with a view to putting my name forward to General as A.D.O.S. L of C North	
	30/3/17.		Routine. Inspected Arms & Clothing of men on parade. I cautioned them about necessity for strict discipline and as to the saluting of Officers and other matters I particularly dwelt on the danger of smoking in Ordnance Dumps.	

2353 Wt. W2544/1454 700,000 5/15 D. D. & L. A.D.S.S./Forms/C. 2118.

Instructions regarding War Diaries and Intelligence Summaries are contained in F. S. Regs., Part II. and the Staff Manual respectively. Title Pages will be prepared in manuscript.

WAR DIARY
or
INTELLIGENCE SUMMARY
(Erase heading not required.)

Army Form C. 2118

Place	Date	Hour	Summary of Events and Information	Remarks and references to Appendices
BAILLEUL	31/3/17		Proceeded to Neuf Berquin with the Staff Captain of the Artillery to inspect the Stores of the D.A.C. to ensure that full stocks of necessary reserves of spares were held. We visited Sections Nos 2 + 3. As Stores were packed for moving I could not personally check them. But I was assured by the Os.C. that full quantities were held or indented for. I found that serviceable parts were being issued to the batteries without any definite check that the "U" parts were returned to Ordnance. I afterwards lunched with the C.R.A and reported the matter to him personally. I also wrote on my return to the C.R.A. so that the matter might have his attention. I also visited the	
			On my return to BAILLEUL some difficulty having arisen as to the occupation by the D.A.D.O.S. of Stores at 190 Rue de la Gare I saw the Camp Commandant of the II Anzac and after his communication with the Town Major it was arranged that the Dump should remain at 190 Rue de la Gare and Offices at 167 Rue de la Gare. On this condition I stated that I was prepared to leave 1 Rue de Poissons. I then proceeded to ARMENTIAIRE to lecture to the 11th Lancs. Fusiliers on [illegible]	

Instructions regarding War Diaries and Intelligence Summaries are contained in F. S. Regs., Part II. and the Staff Manual respectively. Title pages will be prepared in manuscript.

Army Form C. 2118.

WAR DIARY or INTELLIGENCE SUMMARY. D.A.D.O.S. 25 Division

(Erase heading not required.)

Vol 17

Place	Date	Hour	Summary of Events and Information	Remarks and references to Appendices
BAILLEUL	1/4/17 2/4/17		Routine work	
	3/4/17.		Proceeded to MERRIS to discuss the question of the return of winter clothing with the A.A. & Q.M.G. I then visited Hd. Qrs. of the 75 Infty Bde and saw Brig. General Baird the G.O.C. the Brigade. He made no complaint as to Ordnance Services. The A.D.O.S. II Anzacs inspected my Offices and Dump at Bailleul and expressed himself as satisfied.	
	4/4/17		The D.O.S. inspected Ordnance Dump BAILLEUL.	
	5/4/17.		Proceeded to neighbourhood of La SEULE endeavouring to find a suitable place for a Dump for winter clothing. After much searching found an empty farm near Rd RABOT. I instructed Salvage Officer to take possession of it and prepare it. I reported my action to A.D.O.S. II Anzacs and A.A.Q.M.G. 25 Dn.	
	6/4/17		Routine.	

2353 Wt. W2544/1454 700,000 5/15 D. D. & L. A.D.S.S./Forms/C. 2118.

Instructions regarding War Diaries and Intelligence Summaries are contained in F. S. Regs., Part II. and the Staff Manual respectively. Title pages will be prepared in manuscript.

WAR DIARY
or
INTELLIGENCE SUMMARY.
(*Erase heading not required.*)

D.A.D.O.S.
25 Division

Army Form C. 2118.

Place	Date	Hour	Summary of Events and Information	Remarks and references to Appendices
BAILLEUL	7/4/17.		Routine	
	8/4/17		Proceeded to NEUF BERQUIN for general supervision & brought back Senior N.C.O. to put him in charge at Ordnance Dump, 1 Rue des Poissons.	
	9/4/17		Proceeded to STEENJE and lectured to Officers of 2 Royal Irish Rifles on Ordnance Services.	
	10/4/17		Routine.	
	11/4/17		Inspected Reserve Stores of 74 Machine Gun Co and called on Staff Captains of 7th and 75th Infantry Brigades on Ordnance Services generally.	
	12/4/17.		Attended Conference at A.D.O.S. II Anzac Corps. Visited ~~25th~~ Mobile Veterinary Section and discussed with O.C. & A.D.V.S. the possibility of steeping Hay Nets in various mixtures with a view to preventing horses & mules eating them.	
	13/4/17		Visited 200 & 201 Co. A.S.C. 75th Machine Gun Co. 8th Lancs. and 10th Cheshires with A.D.V.S. to enquire into the question of the life of Hay Nets and Nose Bags. I suggested experiments in steeping the hay nets before issue in a mixture of Creosote & Tar in the ration of 1 to 20 of water.	

2353 Wt. W2544/1454 700,000 5/15 D. D. & L. A.D.S.S./Forms/C. 2118.

Army Form C. 2118.

Instructions regarding War Diaries and Intelligence Summaries are contained in F. S. Regs., Part II. and the Staff Manual respectively. Title pages will be prepared in manuscript.

WAR DIARY
or
INTELLIGENCE SUMMARY.
(Erase heading not required.)

Place	Date	Hour	Summary of Events and Information	Remarks and references to Appendices
BAILLEUL	14/4/17		Visited A, B + C Batteries of 110th Bde Artillery with A.D.V.S and Staff Captain. In B/110 I found no Shoemaker or Tailor and no arrangements for the repair of haynets. I reported this to C.R.A. pointing out consequent wastage of public money. In C/110 I found Officers Boots being repaired free. I pointed out the irregularity & informed "Q" that a D.R.O. preventing the practice might be published. In my absence the A.D.O.S. II Anzac visited my Office and looked through outstanding Indents for gun parts. I had already done this and had forwarded to him a complete list for hastening action.	
	15/4/17		Routine	
	16/4/17		A.D.O.S. II Anzac inspected outstanding Infantry Indents to discover important shortages.	
	17/4/17		Went to MERVILLE with A.D.V.S. with a view to a contract for the making of Hay nets. As it appeared that any contract placed in Merville would in fact be replaced by the local contractor in Paris and as the amount of money involved was rather large I referred the matter to the A.D.O.S. II Anzac that an Army Contract might be considered for the Corps or Army.	

2353 Wt. W2544/1454 700,000 5/15 D. D. & L. A.D.S.S./Forms/C. 2118.

Instructions regarding War Diaries and Intelligence Summaries are contained in F. S. Regs., Part II. and the Staff Manual respectively. Title pages will be prepared in manuscript.

WAR DIARY
or
INTELLIGENCE SUMMARY.
(Erase heading not required.)

Army Form C. 2118.

Place	Date	Hour	Summary of Events and Information	Remarks and references to Appendices
BAILLEUL	18/4/17		Routine.	
	19/4/17.		Lectured to Adjutants at Divisional School LA MOTTE on Ordnance Services. Went to HAZEBROUCK to purchase paint and Cloth for urgent services in the Division.	
	20/4/17		Attended Conference at A.D.O.S. II Anzac Corps	
	21/4/17		Proceeded with A.D.V.S. & Staff Captain Artillery to visit the Batteries of 112th Bde R.F.A. & No 3 Section D.A.C. Found that in several batteries there were no Farriers or Shoemakers and that in consequence much avoidable waste was being incurred. I reported matter to Q. Owing to the shortage of bayonets I asked for 4 fatigue men capable of making nets and started a small Divisional Shop for the purpose. To reduce the cost I am using all the string which comes up from base. In the afternoon I received instructions to proceed to D.D.O.S. L of C. A. on being relieved by Lieut. Evans.	
	22/4/17		Routine.	

2353 Wt. W2544/1454 700,000 5/15 D. D. & L. A.D.S.S./Forms/C. 2118.

Instructions regarding War Diaries and Intelligence Summaries are contained in F. S. Regs., Part II. and the Staff Manual respectively. Title pages will be prepared in manuscript.

WAR DIARY
or
INTELLIGENCE SUMMARY.
(Erase heading not required.)

D. A. D. O. S.
25 Division.

Army Form C. 2118.

Place	Date	Hour	Summary of Events and Information	Remarks and references to Appendices
BAILLEUL	23/4/17		Lieut EAGLES A.O.D. reported to take over duty as D A D O S of the Division on my receiving orders to report for duty with D.D.O.S. St. OMER.	
	24/4/17 25/4/17 26/4/17		Routine + introducing Lt. Eagles into general working of Ordnance Services in the Division	
	27/4/17		Visited 2/25 T. M. Battery + was informed by O.C. that on several occasions owing to lack of transport he had left clothing and technical stores behind on being ordered to move. I went at once to D. T. M. O. and reported the matter and asked him to enquire ~~into the~~ as to the facts.	
	28/4/17		Handed over Imprest A/c, Secret documents, codes, records etc to Lt Eagles in preparation for ~~giving up~~ handing over duties of D A D O S to him on 29/4/17.	

* above was prepared by Capt Stewart Wallace.

2353 Wt. W2544/1454 700,000 5/15 D. D. & L. A.D.S.S./Forms/C. 2118.

Instructions regarding War Diaries and Intelligence Summaries are contained in F. S. Regs., Part II. and the Staff Manual respectively. Title pages will be prepared in manuscript.

WAR DIARY
or
INTELLIGENCE SUMMARY.
(Erase heading not required.)

Army Form C. 2118.

DADOS
25th Division

Place	Date	Hour	Summary of Events and Information	Remarks and references to Appendices
BAILLEUL	29/4/17		Commenced duties of DADOS in place of Capt Stewart Wallace. Routine work chiefly	
	30/4/17		Capt Stewart Wallace left Division for duty on L of C under DDOS North. Arrangements made with O.O. I Anzac Corps Troops for return to him of any tentage in the event of a divisional move.	
			Visited AA&QMG at 9.30 pm. & discussed Winter Clothing return. Everything apparently satisfactory except the unavoidable shortage of certain Ordnance stores.	

30/4/17 A C H [illegible] Lt.
DADOS
25th Division

2353 Wt. W2544/1454 700,000 5/15 D. D. & L. A.D.S.S./Forms/C. 2118.

Instructions regarding War Diaries and Intelligence Summaries are contained in F. S. Regs., Part II. and the Staff Manual respectively. Title pages will be prepared in manuscript.

WAR DIARY
or
INTELLIGENCE SUMMARY.
(*Erase heading not required.*)

D.A.D.O.S.
25th Division

Army Form C. 2118.

Vol 18

Place	Date	Hour	Summary of Events and Information	Remarks and references to Appendices
BAILLEUL	29/4/17		Took over duties of D.A.D.O.S. from Capt Stewart Wallace.	
	30/4/17		Capt Stewart Wallace left Division for duty under D.D.O.S. L of C. North. Proceeded to Croix du Bac to arrange return of tentage to O.O. II Anzac Corps Troops. Routine work & daily visit to "Q".	
	1/5/17		Proceeded to the divisional Winter Clothing Dump together with the Salvage Officer & the Railhead Ordnance Officer to examine clothing returned by units. The clothing examined seemed to be in a good condition and was fit for reissue at once. Office work generally.	
	2/5/17		Called on 13th Cheshire Regt & 6th South Wales Borderers to enquire into matter of troops obtaining clean clothing on taking baths. They were quite satisfied that their men got a frequent change.	
	3/5/17		Routine work	
	4/5/17		Attended inspection of units of 75th Brigade by the Brigade Commander and the AA & QMG. The inspection was to ascertain the condition of men's equipment	

2353 Wt. W2544/1454 700,000 5/15 D. D. & L. A.D.S.S./Forms/C. 2118.

Instructions regarding War Diaries and Intelligence Summaries are contained in F. S. Regs., Part II. and the Staff Manual respectively. Title pages will be prepared in manuscript.

WAR DIARY
or
INTELLIGENCE SUMMARY.
(*Erase heading not required.*)

D.A.D.O.S
25th Division

Army Form C. 2118.

Place	Date	Hour	Summary of Events and Information	Remarks and references to Appendices
BAILLEUL	5/5/17		Visited units of 7th Brigade with AA&QMG to inspect equipment.	
	6/5/17		Routine work.	
			Visited Railhead and Winter clothing dump.	
	7/5/17		Routine work.	
	9/5/17		Proceeded to Quelmes, Setques & Esquerdes to look up 7th Brigade units.	
			Informed by H.Q. that everything was satisfactory regarding Ordnance Stores.	
	10/5/17		Office work generally; visited winter clothing dump & Salvage.	
			Conference of D.A.D.O.S at Corps.	
	11/5/17		Office & general routine work.	
	12/5/17		Visited several units and proceeded to Hazebrouck, Estaires, Merville on local purchase	
	13/5/17		Routine work	
	14/5/17		– do –	
	15/5/17		Car back from Workshops after 6 days repairs. Proceeded with A.D.V.S to St. Omer on local purchase enquiries.	

2353 Wt. W2544/1454 700,000 5/15 D. D. & L. A.D.S.S./Forms/C. 2118.

Instructions regarding War Diaries and Intelligence Summaries are contained in F. S. Regs., Part II. and the Staff Manual respectively. Title Pages will be prepared in manuscript.

WAR DIARY
or
INTELLIGENCE SUMMARY
(Erase heading not required.)

DADOS
25th Div

Army Form C. 2118

Place	Date	Hour	Summary of Events and Information	Remarks and references to Appendices
BAILLEUL	16/5/17		General work in dump + office. Visited railhead + winter clothing dump.	
	17/5/17		Proceeded to Hazebrouck + Aire on local purchase enquiries. Conference at Corps.	
	18/5/17		Visited No 3 Sect. DAG, 198, 199, 200 Coys ASC.	
	19/5/17		Made arrangements for Divisional Tentage issue.	
	20/5/17		Visited Setques, and closed down my dump on 7th Brigade again moving forward.	
	21/5/17		General Office + Routine work. Interviewed Y.O.M. to take over new store.	
	22/5/17		Routine work. Visited Winter Clothing Dump. Remainder of clothing being despatched to Railhead forthwith.	
	23/5/17		Routine work. Conference at A.D.OS Office, Corps.	
	24/5/17		Routine work	
	25/5/17		— do —	
	26/5/17		— do —	

1875 Wt. W593/826 1,000,000 4/15 J.B.C. & A. A.D.S.S./Forms/C. 2118.

Instructions regarding War Diaries and Intelligence Summaries are contained in F. S. Regs., Part II. and the Staff Manual respectively. Title Pages will be prepared in manuscript.

WAR DIARY
or
INTELLIGENCE SUMMARY
(Erase heading not required.)

DADOS 25th Div.

Army Form C. 2118

Place	Date	Hour	Summary of Events and Information	Remarks and references to Appendices
BAILLEUL	27/5/17		Took over new store from D.O.M.	
	28/5/17		All stores removed from old store and [illegible] store into above. General Routine work	
	29/5/17		Visited Merville to arrange local purchase of Yukon packs.	
	30/5/17		Office work and general arrangements of store distribution	
	31/5/17		Visited Calais Ordnance depot to bring back urgent stores for Divisional Artillery.	

1/6/17 ACA [illegible] Lieut DADOS 25th Div

1875 Wt. W593/826 1,000,000 4/15 J.B.C. & A. A.D.S.S./Forms/C. 2118.

Instructions regarding War Diaries and Intelligence Summaries are contained in F. S. Regs., Part II. and the Staff Manual respectively. Title Pages will be prepared in manuscript.

WAR DIARY
or
INTELLIGENCE SUMMARY
(Erase heading not required.)

DADOS
25th Division

Vol 19

Army Form C. 2118

Place	Date	Hour	Summary of Events and Information	Remarks and references to Appendices
BAILLEUL	1/6/17		General Office work. Manufacture of Artillery flags.	
	2/6/17		Visited Merville to bring back 100 Yukon packs.	
	3/6/17		General Routine work. Local purchases at Merville & Hazebrouck	
	4/6/17		Completion of Yukon pack Manufacture. Arrangements with Salvage that all Winter Clothing is returned at once. Forward Dump opened at Fort Pinkie for supplying urgent wants of units in action	
	5/6/17		Office & General Work.	
	6/6/17		All special & urgent Stores delivered to Units for immediate use. 750 water tins filled delivered to Souvenir Farm.	
	7/6/17		Active operations commenced which are understood at the moment to be highly successful. 1500 galls of water delivered to Mobile Pack Coy	
	8/6/17		General Office Work. Visited Merville & Hazebrouck for bill payments.	

1875 Wt. W593/826 1,000,000 4/15 J.B.C. & A. A.D.S.S./Forms/C. 2118.

Instructions regarding War Diaries and Intelligence Summaries are contained in F. S. Regs., Part II. and the Staff Manual respectively. Title Pages will be prepared in manuscript.

WAR DIARY
or
INTELLIGENCE SUMMARY
(Erase heading not required.)

D.A.D.O.S. 25th Div

Army Form C. 2118

Place	Date	Hour	Summary of Events and Information	Remarks and references to Appendices
BAILLEUL	9/6/17		Ordnance Store & office moved from Bailleul to S.17 Central (Divisional H.Q.). with the exception of Armourers & Bootmakers shops.	
RAVELSBURG	10/6/17		Proceeded to Fort Pinkie & 74th Bde H.Q. Everything reported satisfactory.	
	11/6/17		Remaining shops at Bailleul moved to S.17 Central as above.	
	12/6/17		Proceeded to Strazeele to R.E. Dump; Car sent to shops for a week for repairs. Captured trophies (Machine Guns, trench mortars & trench howitzers) being sent in from units.	
	13/6/17		Above trophies dispatched for exhibition in Square, Bailleul with five field guns in addition.	
	14/6/17		General office work	
	15/6/17		— do —	
	16/6/17		— do —	
	17/6/17		— do —	

1875 Wt. W593/826 1,000,000 4/15 J.B.C. & A. A.D.S.S./Forms/C. 2118.

Instructions regarding War Diaries and Intelligence Summaries are contained in F. S. Regs., Part II. and the Staff Manual respectively. Title Pages will be prepared in manuscript.

WAR DIARY
or
INTELLIGENCE SUMMARY
(Erase heading not required.)

D.A.D.O.S. 25th Division

Army Form C. 2118

Place	Date	Hour	Summary of Events and Information	Remarks and references to Appendices
RAVELSBERG	18/6/17		General Routine work. Arranged for surplus stores + divisional stores to be stored at Div. Store Farm, Bailleul	
	19/6/17		Office work + general arrangements for moving.	
	20/6/17		— do — — do —	
	21/6/17		Attended Corps ordnance Conference with A.D.O.S.	
	22/6/17		Proceeded to Bomy to arrange movement of office and store thereto.	
			Special stores, for operations used in Messines advance returned to Ordnance Officer II ANZAC Corps Troops.	
	23/6/17		All Railhead Stores taken direct to Bomy to await arrival of Division	
	24/6/17		Remainder of Camp Equipment returned to O.O. II ANZAC. Corps Troops. Office, stores + personnel moved from Ravelsberg to Bomy.	

1875 Wt. W593/826 1,000,000 4/15 J.B.C. & A. A.D.S.S./Forms/C. 2118.

Instructions regarding War Diaries and Intelligence Summaries are contained in F. S. Regs., Part II. and the Staff Manual respectively. Title Pages will be prepared in manuscript.

WAR DIARY
or
INTELLIGENCE SUMMARY

(Erase heading not required.)

D.A.D.O.S
25th Division

Army Form C. 2118

Place	Date	Hour	Summary of Events and Information	Remarks and references to Appendices
BOMY.	25/6/17		Visited Ravelsberg to give instructions as to stores to be sent from old camp to Divisions + Formation to whom our Artillery, REs + Pioneer Bttn are being attached.	
			Called on D.D.O.S. 1st Army to receive any instructions required.	
	26/6/17		General office work.	
			Visited Railhead (Lillers) to make necessary arrangements as to method of the issue of vehicles to units and also as to the return of Stores + Salvage.	
	27/6/17		General Office duties.	
	28/6/17		Units visited and found well equipped.	
	29/6/17		General Routine work.	
	30/6/17		Remainder of Units visited and expressed satisfaction as to the meeting by Dept. of their indents.	

4/7/17

A C [illegible] Capt
D.A.D.O.S.
25th Div.

1875 Wt. W593/826 1,000,000 4/15 J.B.C. & A. A.D.S.S./Forms/C. 2118.

Instructions regarding War Diaries and Intelligence Summaries are contained in F. S. Regs., Part II. and the Staff Manual respectively. Title Pages will be prepared in manuscript.

WAR DIARY
or
INTELLIGENCE SUMMARY
(Erase heading not required.)

D.A.D.O.S.
25th Division.

Army Form C. 2118

Vol 20

Place	Date	Hour	Summary of Events and Information	Remarks and references to Appendices
BOMY	1/7/17		D.A.D.O.S. on leave.	
	2/7/17		General Routine work for equipping Division before re-entering the line	
	3/7/17			
	4/7/17		Visited units in Fruges area and made necessary arrangements for issuing stores to 7th Bde while they are attached to 8th Division	
	5/7/17		General office work.	
	6/7/17		— do —. Proceeded to Busseboom with D.A.Q.M.G.	
	7/7/17		Proceeded to 11th Lancs Fusiliers & D.T.M.O. with C.I.O.M. 1st Army to examine Field Kitchens and Stokes mortar.	
	8/7/17		Proceeded to Busseboom to arrange site for stores & office. This was done apparently satisfactorily	
Busseboom area	9/7/17		Office & Stores moved to Poperinge – Reninghelst Road in Busseboom area. Above quoted site already given to ~~[illegible]~~ another unit. Another place found after much difficulty.	

1875 Wt. W593/826 1,000,000 4/15 J.B.C. & A. A.D.S.S./Forms/C. 2118.

Instructions regarding War Diaries and Intelligence Summaries are contained in F. S. Regs., Part II. and the Staff Manual respectively. Title Pages will be prepared in manuscript.

WAR DIARY
or
INTELLIGENCE SUMMARY
(Erase heading not required.)

Army Form C. 2118

Place	Date	Hour	Summary of Events and Information	Remarks and references to Appendices
	10/7/17		Remainder of Stores moved from Bomy, except for 74th Brigade who remained at Bomy for training.	
	11/7/17		General Routine & Office work.	
	12/7/17		— do —	
	13/7/17		Arrangements made with DHQ for 3000 petrol tins to carry water in active operations. SMTO to supply under Army Authority. Visited 201 Coy ASC & HQ Coy.	
	14/7/17		300 Pack Saddles arrived from base to be used chiefly with Divisional Pack Transport Coy.	
	15/7/17		General Routine Work	
	18/7/17		Visited Merville to place contract for the manufacture of special carrier designed by D.A.D.M.S. to bring in wounded on pack animals.	
			Arranged for Divisional Stores to be brought from Depot in Bailleul to present area	

1875 Wt. W593/826 1,000,000 4/15 J.B.C. & A. A.D.S.S./Forms/C. 2118.

Instructions regarding War Diaries and Intelligence Summaries are contained in F. S. Regs., Part II. and the Staff Manual respectively. Title pages will be prepared in manuscript.

WAR DIARY
or
INTELLIGENCE SUMMARY.
(Erase heading not required.)

Army Form C. 2118.

Place	Date	Hour	Summary of Events and Information	Remarks and references to Appendices
Reninghelst area.	19/7/17		Arrangements made for drawing 5.000 gallons of water in petrol tanks from Water point No 2 & 3. General Office Work	
	20/7/17		Visited Divisional Baths. Collected special carriers for wounded from Merville.	
	21/7/17		Proceeded to Divisional Store, Bailleul for Special luminous paint for night work. From here went on to Divisional Reinforcement Camp at Millam. This camp is supplied by VIII Corps Ordnance whilst in that area.	
	22/7/17		General Routine Work.	
	23/7/17		Ordered by D.H.Q. to move near to them on 25th Inst. Site found & arrangements made. 1000 petrol tins filled with drinking water despatched & delivered to K. dump	
	24/7/17		Visited 2nd Australian Supply Column & Divisional Store for dug out lamps. 1000 more petrol tins filled despatched & delivered to K dump.	

2353 Wt. W2544/1454 700,000 5/15 D. D. & L. A.D.S.S./Forms/C. 2118.

Instructions regarding War Diaries and Intelligence Summaries are contained in F. S. Regs., Part II. and the Staff Manual respectively. Title pages will be prepared in manuscript.

WAR DIARY
or
INTELLIGENCE SUMMARY.
(*Erase heading not required.*)

D.O.D.O.S 25th Div.

Army Form C. 2118.

Place	Date	Hour	Summary of Events and Information	Remarks and references to Appendices
Busseboom area	25/7/17		Conference with Staff Captain at "Q" Office to discuss final arrangement for Ordnance Supplies during the attack. Forward dump of Ordnance Stores was not required. 500 Petrol tins filled with drinking water delivered to K dump.	
	26/7/17		General Routine work.	
	27/7/17		— do — obtained F.S. lamps for Artillery ~~and~~ in lieu of Siege lamps which could not be procured.	
	28/7/17		Visited D.D.O.S 5th Army to bring back compasses magnetic urgently required by Infantry Battns. Scale increased from 32 to 40 per battalion	
	29/7/17		Office work generally. 147 Wheels of sorts received from Base for various transport in Division.	
	30/7/17		Oil lubricating & buffer despatched to K dump for emergency.	
	31/7/17		General Routine work.	

[illegible] Capt
D.A.D.O.S 25th Div

2353 Wt. W2544/1454 700,000 5/15 D. D. & L. A.D.S.S./Forms/C. 2118.

Instructions regarding War Diaries and Intelligence Summaries are contained in F. S. Regs., Part II. and the Staff Manual respectively. Title pages will be prepared in manuscript.

WAR DIARY
or
INTELLIGENCE SUMMARY.
(Erase heading not required.)

Army Form C. 2118.

DADOS
25th Division
Vol 21

Place	Date	Hour	Summary of Events and Information	Remarks and references to Appendices
	1/8/17		Proceeded to Bailleul for purchase of steel rod for manufacture of leg rests for wounded on stretchers. Visited 75th Field Ambulance, who pronounced demands satisfactory.	
	2/8/17		Compasses magnetic issued to division on increased scale of 8 per Battalion making a total of 40 per Bttn.	
	3/8/17		Authority granted for issue of 100 Primus Stoves for use in trenches during wet weather.	
	4/8/17		2500 sets of clothing brought from Base to replace that of 7th & 75th Brigades on coming in from the line. The clothing of these Brigades was in a bad state owing to extremely wet weather which rendered clothes temporarily unserviceable on account of being too soiled & muddy to clean locally.	
	5/8/17		Lorry sent to Base to obtain 100 primus stoves mentioned above which are held for distribution by D.H.Q. - twenty five being for 74th Bde.	
	6/8/17		General Routine work. Visited "K" dump & Salvage Dump.	
	7/8/17		Visited Advanced Reinforcement Camp at Oudezeele & arranged to supply small requirements by Supply lorry. Visited Army H.Q. & 7th Bde at Halifax Camp	

2353/ Wt. W2544/1454 700,000 5/15 D. D. & L. A.D.S.S./Forms/C. 2118.

Instructions regarding War Diaries and Intelligence Summaries are contained in F. S. Regs., Part II. and the Staff Manual respectively. Title pages will be prepared in manuscript.

WAR DIARY
or
INTELLIGENCE SUMMARY.
(Erase heading not required.)

Army Form C. 2118.

Place	Date	Hour	Summary of Events and Information	Remarks and references to Appendices
	8/8/17		General Office work. Issued clothing to units from the line. Car in workshops.	
	9/8/17		Car in workshops under repair. General office work.	
	10/8/17		~~[illegible]~~ Visited units & found that most stores had been received by them with exception of a few items which are difficult to obtain owing to temporary shortage at Base	
	11/8/17 12/8/17 13/8/17		General Office work.	
	14/8/17		Visited Brigades. Obtained equipment from Salvage to refit units now at rest.	
	15/8/17 16/8/17		Spent in going through records and hastening any detail demands outstanding from Base & cancelling outstanding indents that units are not requiring to be fulfilled	

2353 Wt. W2544/1454 700,000 5/15 D. D. & L. A.D.S.S./Forms/C. 2118.

Army Form C. 2118.

WAR DIARY
or
INTELLIGENCE SUMMARY.
(Erase heading not required.)

Instructions regarding War Diaries and Intelligence Summaries are contained in F. S. Regs., Part II. and the Staff Manual respectively. Title pages will be prepared in manuscript.

Place	Date	Hour	Summary of Events and Information	Remarks and references to Appendices
Steenvoorde	17/8/17		Moved to Steenvoorde after making arrangements to supply units in forward area.	
	18/8/17		Visited units of 74th Brigade who were found to be well supplied with all available stores	
	19/8/17		Fixed up dump & office and armourers shops in readiness to make issues immediately.	
	20/8/17		General office work. Visited 75th Machine Gun Coy with D.M.G.O. The Coy found to be short of one or two items such as oil & soft soap which is being obtained for them urgently	
	21/8/17 22/8/17		General Office work	
	23/8/17		Manufactured sample of covers for Lewis & Vickers gun also muzzle protector for rifle and a wooden ski for the prevention of men sinking in mud when crossing swampy ground. These articles have been handed to D.A.Q. for inspection.	

2353 Wt. W2544/1454 700,000 5/15 D. D. & L. A.D.S.S./Forms/C. 2118.

Instructions regarding War Diaries and Intelligence Summaries are contained in F. S. Regs., Part II. and the Staff Manual respectively. Title pages will be prepared in manuscript.

WAR DIARY
or
INTELLIGENCE SUMMARY.
(Erase heading not required.)

Army Form C. 2118.

Place	Date	Hour	Summary of Events and Information	Remarks and references to Appendices
Steenvoorde	24/8/17		General office work	
	25/8/17		Proceeded to Calais to visit the Chief Ordnance Officer to discuss matters of issue. Apparently all effort is being made to procure such articles as revolvers, breast covers, caps, pantaloons etc of which there is a great shortage at the moment. Obtained material for the manufacture of 600 flags for training purposes in the division. N.B. Textile stores very difficult to obtain.	
	26/8/17		Office work.	
	27/8/17		— do — Manufactured another Lewis Gun Carrier for use in taking up into action in wet weather.	
	28/8/17		} General Routine work.	
	29/8/17			
	30/8/17		Visited Heavy Trench Mortar Battery & D.T.M.O. They requested double issue of clothing for men owing to the greasy nature of work	
	31/8/17		General Office work	

31/8/17 A C H [illegible] Capt. S.O. 205

2353 Wt. W2544/1454 700,000 5/15 D. D. & L. A.D.S.S./Forms/C. 2118.

Instructions regarding War Diaries and Intelligence Summaries are contained in F. S. Regs., Part II. and the Staff Manual respectively. Title pages will be prepared in manuscript.

WAR DIARY
or
INTELLIGENCE SUMMARY.
(Erase heading not required.)

Army Form C. 2118.

DADOS 25th Division

Vol 22

Place	Date	Hour	Summary of Events and Information	Remarks and references to Appendices
Steenvoorde	1/9/17		Preparations for move to forward area.	
	2/9/17			
	3/9/17		Moved to Reninghelst and took over dump from D.A.D.O.S. 23rd Div.	
	4/9/17		Moved to original dump at G14 d. Central	
	5/9/17		General Routine work.	
	6/9/17			
	7/9/17		Brigades visited and action taken for immediate requirements & Stores hastened.	
	8/9/17		Proceeded to Labeuvriere for arranging stores & office.	
	9/9/17		Prepared to move & instructions issued for handing over all Corps stores to either relieving division or O.O. Corps. Troops.	
Labeuvriere	10/9/17		Move to Labeuvriere commenced and completed on	
	11/9/17		, one lorry & personnel being left behind to complete return of Corps stores.	

2353 Wt. W2544/1454 700,000 5/15 D. D. & L. A.D.S.S./Forms/C. 2118.

Instructions regarding War Diaries and Intelligence Summaries are contained in F. S. Regs., Part II. and the Staff Manual respectively. Title pages will be prepared in manuscript.

WAR DIARY
or
INTELLIGENCE SUMMARY.
(Erase heading not required.)

DADOS 25th Div.

Army Form C. 2118.

Place	Date	Hour	Summary of Events and Information	Remarks and references to Appendices
Lahenvaine	12/9/17		General arrangements of dump. Visited DDOS 1st Army + ADOS 1st Corps for any special instructions as to procedure in new area. Visited DADOS 46th Division with ADOS.	
	13/9/17		Visited Lillers Railhead to arrange with the Railhead Ordnance Officer + R.T.O. to hold over heavy stores for Artillery until latter arrived in this area.	
			Visited all units of 7th Brigade.	
	14/9/17		Visited all units of 74th Brigade.	
	15/9/17		Handed over to Cond^r Journeaux + issued instructions to be carried out during leave. Proceeded on leave.	
	16th to 26th		During my absence all units of 75th Brigade were visited by my relief. 17.500 blankets were obtained from Base to make the initial issue of 1 per man. Horse rugs were also obtained up to 50 per cent of strength.	

Instructions regarding War Diaries and Intelligence Summaries are contained in F. S. Regs., Part II. and the Staff Manual respectively. Title pages will be prepared in manuscript.

WAR DIARY
or
INTELLIGENCE SUMMARY.
(Erase heading not required.)

Army Form C. 2118.

DADOS
25th Division

Place	Date	Hour	Summary of Events and Information	Remarks and references to Appendices
Lebeaurin	27/9/17		General Office work. 250 Packsaddles collected + stored to awaiting distribution instructions from division.	
	28/9/17		Visited Lillers Railhead and ADOS 1st Corps reference issue of Soyers stoves and water tins for the division.	
	29/9/17		General Routine work.	
	30/9/17		Preparation made for the demand of winter clothing — indents from units to be consolidated.	

A. C. Heagle[?] Capt
DADOS
25th Div
30/9/17

Instructions regarding War Diaries and Intelligence Summaries are contained in F. S. Regs., Part II. and the Staff Manual respectively. Title pages will be prepared in manuscript.

WAR DIARY
or
INTELLIGENCE SUMMARY.
(Erase heading not required.)

Dados
25th Division

Army Form C. 2118.

Vol 23

Place	Date	Hour	Summary of Events and Information	Remarks and references to Appendices
Labeuvrière	Oct 1st		General Routine ~~[illegible]~~ Work.	
	2nd		Visited 195 M.G. Coy re equipment of section moving to another formation.	
	3rd		Office work & preparation for move.	
	4th		Proceeded to Locon to arrange exchange of stores & billets with 2nd Division.	
	5th 6th ~~7~~		Delivered all available stores to units. Moved Armourers shop to Locon.	
Locon	7th		Moved all stores & office to Locon. Move completed.	
	8th		Arranged change of system into Refilling point drawing on first opportunity.	
	9th		Visited XI Corps A.D.O.S. reference requirements of XI Corps Ordnance System	
	10th		General Office work	

2353 Wt. W2544/1454 700,000 5/15 D. D. & L. A.D.S.S./Forms/C. 2118.

Instructions regarding War Diaries and Intelligence Summaries are contained in F. S. Regs., Part II. and the Staff Manual respectively. Title pages will be prepared in manuscript.

WAR DIARY or INTELLIGENCE SUMMARY. (Erase heading not required.)

DADOS 25th Division.

Army Form C. 2118.

Place	Date	Hour	Summary of Events and Information	Remarks and references to Appendices
Locon	11/10/17		All stores collected from Refilling points.	
	12/10/17		Visited all Brigade H.Q., all of whom were satisfied with the demand & issue of stores.	
	13/10/17 } 14/10/17		3400 Gum boots arrived from Base. Distributed to Brigades to make up 1000 per Brigade. Each Brigade to make its own arrangements for storage cleaning & sending to Div Bootmakers shop for repair.	
	15/10/17		General office work and perusal of outstanding indents.	
	16/10/17		2nd Blanket per man received from Base. As many as possible issued direct to Brigades or Units, remainder to be drawn from Refilling Point & Main Dump.	
	17/10/17		Visited Reinforcement Battalion to obtain information as to any special requirements	
	18/10/17 } 19/10/17		General Routine Work	

2353 Wt. W2544/1454 700,000 5/15 D. D. & L. A.D.S.S./Forms/C. 2118.

Instructions regarding War Diaries and Intelligence Summaries are contained in F. S. Regs., Part II. and the Staff Manual respectively. Title pages will be prepared in manuscript.

WAR DIARY
or
INTELLIGENCE SUMMARY.
(Erase heading not required.)

DADOS
9th Div

Army Form C. 2118.

Place	Date	Hour	Summary of Events and Information	Remarks and references to Appendices
Locon	20/10/17 – 21/10/17		First consignment of Winter Clothing arrived. Drawers Woollen issued to Batts. Vests issued direct to Units as well as F.S. Boots.	
	22/10/17		Visited 7th Brigade HQ + Brigade Bomb Dump with Corps Ammunition Officer.	
	23/10/17 – 24/10/17		General Office + Routine Work	
	25/10/17		Car returned from shops after a month away. Visited La Gorgue Railhead to arrange with RO.O to hold up various stores for use in Division. Visited D.O.M. Merville (No 12 Shop) + obtained 60 [illegible] for Divisional use.	
	26/10/17		Office work	
	27/10/17		Visited 4 Bttns of 7th Bde. Stock of clothing found in 3 Stores.	
	28/10/17		~~Visited~~ Car again sent to shop for complete overhaul. Office work.	
	29/10/17		100 Hot food Containers received from Base together with a consignment of Leather Jerkins.	
	30/10/17		Conference at le Quesnoy Chateau of ADOS, Staff Capts, O.C. Train + QMS of Division	
	31/10/17		Visited D.O. XI Corps Troops at Bethune; also made local purchases in same town	

A. C. H. [illegible] Capt DADOS

2353 Wt. W2544/1454 700,000 5/15 D. D. & L. A.D.S.S./Forms/C. 2118.

Instructions regarding War Diaries and Intelligence Summaries are contained in F. S. Regs., Part II. and the Staff Manual respectively. Title pages will be prepared in manuscript.

WAR DIARY or INTELLIGENCE SUMMARY.

(Erase heading not required.)

Army Form C. 2118.

DADOS 25th Div.

Vol 24

Place	Date	Hour	Summary of Events and Information	Remarks and references to Appendices
LOCON	1/11/17		General Routine work	
	2/11/17		Visited ADOS Corps and thence to H.Q. Coy A.S.C.	
	3/11/17		Visited 75th Brigade H.Q. & found no shortage of serious nature	
	4/11/17		General Office & Routine work	
	5/11/17			
	6/11/17		Visited units of 75th Brigade reference stock held in QM store. Meeting of Quartermasters Salvage Office & DADOS proposed	
	7/11/17		Local Purchase in Bethune ~~& Merville~~	
	8/11/17		Obtained 60 mud scrapers from No 21 Ordnance Mobile Workshop. Also visited Gun Park at Hersin to arrange about collection of Gun stores.	

2353 Wt. W2544/1454 700,000 5/15 D. D. & L. A.D.S.S./Forms/C. 2118.

Instructions regarding War Diaries and Intelligence Summaries are contained in F. S. Regs., Part II. and the Staff Manual respectively. Title pages will be prepared in manuscript.

WAR DIARY
or
INTELLIGENCE SUMMARY.
(Erase heading not required.)

Army Form C. 2118.

Place	Date	Hour	Summary of Events and Information	Remarks and references to Appendices
Locon	9/11/17		Meeting of DADOS, Salvage Officer + Quartermaster at Le Quesnoy Chateau. It was decided that units should render a return on 27th day of each month showing ~~stores~~ the following stores received from Ordnance Trousers, Jackets, Pantaloons, Mess Tins, Greatcoats, Caps etc and also showing number returned by this replacement to Salvage, at the same time attaching Salvage Receipt.	
	10/11/17		General Office work	
	11/11/17		Visited 7th Bde HQ + units with Staff Capt.	
	12/11/17		Visited Railhead Ordnance Officer la Gorgue + arranged for serviceable equipment to be saved for me	
	13/11/17		General Office work.	
	14/11/17			
	15/11/17			
	16/11/17		150 Yukon Packs received from Base + kept in store at Disposal of DHQ	

2353 Wt. W2544/1454 700,000 5/15 D. D. & L. A.D.S.S./Forms/C. 2118.

Instructions regarding War Diaries and Intelligence Summaries are contained in F. S. Regs., Part II. and the Staff Manual respectively. Title pages will be prepared in manuscript.

WAR DIARY
or
INTELLIGENCE SUMMARY.
(Erase heading not required.)

Army Form C. 2118.

Place	Date	Hour	Summary of Events and Information	Remarks and references to Appendices
Locon	17/11/17		Proceeded to 6th S.W. Borderers to arranged about the supply of Band instruments which were originally left at Base on the unit being ordered forward. Army authority given for issue of stores for which receipt had been given by Ordnance but the remainder had to be paid for by Batn	
	18/11/17		Visited Bethune, Lillers & Aire to obtain quotations & probable manufacture of red brow bands for horses.	
	19/11/17		General Office work	
	20/11/17		– do –	
	21/11/17		Experimented with different shades of Khaki blanco to obtain one common colour for all units in division who are entitled to Web equipment	

2353 Wt. W2544/1454 700,000 5/15 D. D. & L. A.D.S.S./Forms/C. 2118.

Instructions regarding War Diaries and Intelligence Summaries are contained in F. S. Regs., Part II. and the Staff Manual respectively. Title pages will be prepared in manuscript.

WAR DIARY
or
INTELLIGENCE SUMMARY.
(Erase heading not required.)

Army Form C. 2118.

Place	Date	Hour	Summary of Events and Information	Remarks and references to Appendices
Locon	22/11/17 23/11/17		General Office work. Issued certain orders of discipline to all ranks with D.A.D.O.S.	
	24/11/17		New cook house & dining shed started for personnel	
	25/11/17		Visited Therouanne with D.A.Q.M.G.	
	26/11/17		Move orders to Bomy area. Visited Bomy, Ganippe, Lisbourg & Lilbus to obtain a site for Stores & Offices	
	27/11/17 28/11/17		Preparation for move	
Bomy	29/11/17		Moved to Bomy. Stores arranged for in Theatre.	
	30/11/17		General Routine work	

30/11/17 [signature] Capt. D.A.D.O.S. 25 Div.

2353 Wt. W2544/1454 700,000 5/15 D. D. & L. A.D.S.S./Forms/C. 2118.

Army Form C. 2118.

Instructions regarding War Diaries and Intelligence Summaries are contained in F. S. Regs., Part II. and the Staff Manual respectively. Title pages will be prepared in manuscript.

WAR DIARY
or
INTELLIGENCE SUMMARY.
(Erase heading not required.)

DADOS 25th Division

Vol 25

Place	Date	Hour	Summary of Events and Information	Remarks and references to Appendices
Bomy	1/12/17		Visited Railhead and No 12 Ordnance Mobile Workshop.	
	2/12/17		Proceeded to St Pol to arrange trucks for move of ordnance stores & personnel	
	3/12/17		Stores despatched as above to Achiet le petit.	
Achiet le Petit	4/12/17		Moved to Achiet le Petit.	
Grevillers	5/12/17		Moved to Grevillers.	
	6/12/17		Visited DADOS 3rd division to arrange supply of ordnance to 74th Brigade + Divisional Artillery.	
	7/12/17		General office work	
	8/12/17		Proceeded to Amiens on Local Purchase of Electric Lamp bulbs	
	9/12/17		General Office Work	
	10/12/17		— do —	
	11/12/17		Visited R.A. Headquarters to arrange supply of two howitzer deficient on leaving last Army.	

2353 Wt. W2544/1454 700,000 5/15 D. D. & L. A.D.S.S./Forms/C. 2118.

Army Form C. 2118.

Instructions regarding War Diaries and Intelligence Summaries are contained in F. S. Regs., Part II. and the Staff Manual respectively. Title pages will be prepared in manuscript.

WAR DIARY
or
INTELLIGENCE SUMMARY.

(Erase heading not required.)

Place	Date	Hour	Summary of Events and Information	Remarks and references to Appendices
Gavillers	12/12/17		Proceeded to Favreuil to arrange taking over dumps & offices from DADOS 3rd Division. Proceeded to Amiens to purchase 10.000 metres of tape for CRE.	
	13/12/17		Armourers shop moved to Favreuil.	
	14/12/17		Bulk clothing & other stores — do —	
Favreuil	15/12/17		Move completed.	
	16/12/17		Proceeded to Amiens on Local Purchase	
	17/12/17		Visited S.A.A. dump and arranged for tarpaulins to cover ammunition.	
	18/12/17		General Routine work. Visited 76th Field Ambulance.	
	19/12/17		Visited Railhead and 4th Corps H.Q.	
	20/12/17 21/12/17		} General Office work.	

2353 Wt. W2544/1454 700,000 5/15 D. D. & L. A.D.S.S./Forms/C. 2118.

Instructions regarding War Diaries and Intelligence Summaries are contained in F. S. Regs., Part II. and the Staff Manual respectively. Title pages will be prepared in manuscript.

WAR DIARY
or
INTELLIGENCE SUMMARY.
(Erase heading not required.)

Army Form C. 2118.

DADOS 21st Div

Place	Date	Hour	Summary of Events and Information	Remarks and references to Appendices
Favreuil	22/12/17		Proceeded to Doullens on Local Purchase.	
	23/12/17		Proceeded to Albert to obtain stores for 13th Cheshire & division	
	24/12/17		General Routine Work.	
	25/12/17		— do —	
	26/12/17		Visited DAC & Artillery.	
	27/12/17		Visited ADOS IV Corps re promotion & recommendations	
	28/12/17		Visited 76th Field Ambulance. General Routine Work	
	29/12/17		Proceeded to Frémicourt re issue of Water Cart to 6th South Wales Borderers.	

2353 Wt. W2544/1454 700,000 5/15 D. D. & L. A.D.S.S./Forms/C. 2118.

Instructions regarding War Diaries and Intelligence Summaries are contained in F. S. Regs., Part II. and the Staff Manual respectively. Title pages will be prepared in manuscript.

WAR DIARY
or
INTELLIGENCE SUMMARY.
(Erase heading not required.)

DADOS
25th Div

Army Form C. 2118.

Place	Date	Hour	Summary of Events and Information	Remarks and references to Appendices
Favreuil	30/12/17		General Routine Work. Visited 76th Field Ambulance & checked stores to be held under GRO for Div Rest Station.	
	31/12/17		Visited A.D.O.S IV Corps re howitzer & 18 pounders due to 25th Div Artillery.	

31/12/17 [signature] Capt
DADOS
25th Div

2353 Wt. W2544/1454 700,000 5/15 D. D. & L. A.D.S.S./Forms/C. 2118.

Army Form C. 2118.

Instructions regarding War Diaries and Intelligence Summaries are contained in F. S. Regs., Part II. and the Staff Manual respectively. Title pages will be prepared in manuscript.

WAR DIARY
or
INTELLIGENCE SUMMARY.
(Erase heading not required.)

DADOS 25th Div Vol 21

Place	Date	Hour	Summary of Events and Information	Remarks and references to Appendices
Favreuil	1/1/18		Arranged for 30 more tents to be sent to Store (15 from 75th Bde + 15 from SAA Sec. DAC. Visited Albert on Local Purchase.	
	2/1/18		Visited Transport lines + QM Stores of all infantry units with DAQMG.	
	3/1/18		General Routine Work. Four Vickers Guns overhauled for 7th MG Coy	
	4/1/18		Visited Sapignies + Favreuil Areas.	
	5/1/18 6/1/18		General Office Work. Arrangements made for road to be made in Ordnance Dump. 4 Vickers Guns overhauled for 74th MG Coy	
	7/1/18		500 prs of Gum Boots received for Division	
	8/1/18		General Office Work. Four Vickers Guns overhauled for 74th MG Coy.	
	9/1/18		Visited Amiens on Local Purchase.	

2353 Wt. W2544/1454 700,000 5/15 D. D. & L. A.D.S.S./Forms/C. 2118.

Instructions regarding War Diaries and Intelligence Summaries are contained in F. S. Regs., Part II. and the Staff Manual respectively. Title pages will be prepared in manuscript.

WAR DIARY
or
INTELLIGENCE SUMMARY.
(Erase heading not required.)

Army Form C. 2118.

Place	Date	Hour	Summary of Events and Information	Remarks and references to Appendices
Favreuil	10/1/18		General Office work	
	11/1/18		Roadway commenced in Ordnance dump.	
	12/1/18		General Routine Work	
	13/1/18			
	14/1/18		Visited Heavy Mobile workshops at Albert Visited R.O.O. Bapaume.	
	15/1/18		Visited Arsenes [illegible] on Local Purchase.	
	16/1/18		General Routine Work	
	17/1/18			
	18/1/18		Visited Amiens on local Purchase also Divisional Rest Billet	
	19/1/18		2000 Gum Boots Thigh received from Base Visited A.D.O.S. IV Corps. Arrangements for return of Oat Sacks.	

2353 Wt. W2544/1454 700,000 5/15 D. D. & L. A.D.S.S./Forms/C. 2118.

Instructions regarding War Diaries and Intelligence Summaries are contained in F. S. Regs., Part II. and the Staff Manual respectively. Title pages will be prepared in manuscript.

WAR DIARY
or
INTELLIGENCE SUMMARY.
(Erase heading not required.)

Army Form C. 2118.

Place	Date	Hour	Summary of Events and Information	Remarks and references to Appendices
Favreuil	20/1/18		Arranged for Collection of all Oat Sacks possible. 306 9 Sacks collected. Visited Workshops at Albert.	
	21/1/18		Visited Amiens on local purchase of Lamp glasses & Special Baskets for M.G. Coy.	
	22/1/18		General Routine Work and arrangement of Camp.	
	23/1/18		— do — Returned 200 tents to Corps	
	24/1/18		— do — Returned 50 tents to Corps.	
	25/1/18		Visited I.O.M. 28 + 45 Ordnance Workshops to arrange manufacture of 101 Screw Stops for Mark IV Tripod mounting Vickers	
	26/1/18		Visited D.A.D.O.S 51st Division and A.D.O.S IV Corps.	
	27/1/18		General Routine Work	
	28/1/18		Visited 76th Field Ambulance to check stock held by them as Dressing Station under G.R.O. 2921	

2353 Wt. W2544/1454 700,000 5/15 D. D. & L. A.D.S.S./Forms/C. 2118.

Instructions regarding War Diaries and Intelligence Summaries are contained in F. S. Regs., Part II. and the Staff Manual respectively. Title pages will be prepared in manuscript.

Army Form C. 2118.

WAR DIARY
or
INTELLIGENCE SUMMARY.
(Erase heading not required.)

Place	Date	Hour	Summary of Events and Information	Remarks and references to Appendices
Favreuil	29/1/18		General Routine work. Visited O.O. Army Troops Albert.	
	30/1/18		Proceeding on leave; Cond^r C Journeaux to act during my absence	

A C [illegible] Capt
DADOS
21st Div

2353 Wt. W2544/1454 700,000 5/15 D. D. & L. A.D.S.S./Forms/C. 2118.

Instructions regarding War Diaries and Intelligence Summaries are contained in F. S. Regs., Part II. and the Staff Manual respectively. Title pages will be prepared in manuscript.

WAR DIARY
or
INTELLIGENCE SUMMARY.
(Erase heading not required.)

Army Form C. 2118.

DADOS
25th Division.

Vol 27

Place	Date	Hour	Summary of Events and Information	Remarks and references to Appendices
Sheet 57.C. H.15C.3.6	1/2/18	–	General Routine.	
	2.2.18		General Routine. Visited IV Corps Troops and 1.O.M. 28–115 B'shops.	
	3.2.18		General Routine. Stores handed in by 13 Cheshires on being disbanded	
	4.2.18		General Routine. Stores handed in by 8 South Lancs and 13 Cheshires on being disbanded. Visited Div Stores at Achiet Le Petit and IV Corps Troops.	
	5.2.18		General Routine stores returned by 13 Cheshires & 8th Lancs on being disbanded	
	6.2.18		General Routine. A.D.O.S. visited Divl Dump and offices.	
	7.2.18		General Routine visited 51 Division in contemplation of relieving formation.	
	8.2.18		General Routine Visited 6 Division re arrangements for handing over stores etc to them on being relieved.	
	9.2.18		General Routine Visited DADOS 6 Div re forthcoming move.	

2353 Wt. W2344/1454 700,000 5/15 D. D. & L. A.D.S.S./Forms/C. 2118.

Instructions regarding War Diaries and Intelligence Summaries are contained in F. S. Regs., Part II. and the Staff Manual respectively. Title pages will be prepared in manuscript.

WAR DIARY
or
INTELLIGENCE SUMMARY.
(Erase heading not required.)

Army Form C. 2118.

Place	Date	Hour	Summary of Events and Information	Remarks and references to Appendices
Sheet 57C H15 C.3-6	10/2/18		General Routine. Visited ADOS IV Corps. Handing in of equipt by units being disbanded completed. 8 Lewis M Guns received for Arty units for A.A. defence.	
	11/2/18		General Routine.	
	12.2.18		General Routine. Commenced moving stores to Achiet Le Petit.	
Achiet-Le Petit.	13.2.18		Completed move to Achiet-Le-Petit, relieved DADOS 51 Division. Relieved at H15 C.3-6. Sheet 57C by DADOS 6 Division. General Routine.	
— " —	14.2.18		General Routine.	
— " —	15.2.18		DADOS returned from leave. General arrangement in new dump.	
	16.2.18		General Routine & Office work.	

2353 Wt. W2544/1454 700,000 5/15 D. D. & L. A.D.S.S./Forms/C. 2118.

Instructions regarding War Diaries and Intelligence Summaries are contained in F. S. Regs., Part II. and the Staff Manual respectively. Title pages will be prepared in manuscript.

WAR DIARY
or
INTELLIGENCE SUMMARY.
(Erase heading not required.)

Army Form C. 2118.

DADOS
25th Division

Place	Date	Hour	Summary of Events and Information	Remarks and references to Appendices
Achiet le petit	17/2/18		Visited R.O.D. Achiet le Grand & DADOS 6th Division to obtain items of Web equipment required by 2nd S. Lancs. Visited 6th South Wales Borderers. All satisfactory	
	18/2/18		General Routine Work.	
	19/2/18		Proceeded to Amiens on local purchase duty of Glue, chain etc.	
	20/2/18		Visited 74th Bde H.Q. & 75th Field Ambulance	
	21/2/18		Visited Artillery H.Q at Bouzincourt & Divisional Schools at Couin.	
	22/2/18		General Routine Work.	
	23/2/18		Proceeded to Amiens on purchase of Glue, Lamp Glasses & trophies for Division	
	24/2/18		Visited 74th Bde H.Q. & M.Gun Battalion.	

2353 Wt. W2544/1454 700,000 5/15 D. D. & L. A.D.S.S./Forms/C. 2118.

Instructions regarding War Diaries and Intelligence Summaries are contained in F. S. Regs., Part II. and the Staff Manual respectively. Title pages will be prepared in manuscript.

WAR DIARY
or
INTELLIGENCE SUMMARY.
(*Erase heading not required.*)

Army Form C. 2118.

DADOS 25th Division.

Place	Date	Hour	Summary of Events and Information	Remarks and references to Appendices
Achiet le petit	25/2/18		Proceeded to Amiens to bring away Tarpaulins purchased by Division. Visited 112 Bde HQ at Manlté.	
	26/2/18		General Routine work. Visited RDO Achiet le Grand to arrange supply of pistols. 375 Tarpaulins arrived from Base.	
	27/2/18		General Office & Routine work. Arrangements made for return of surplus equipment from Pioneer Btln. DDOS called at office & dump.	
	28/2/18		General Office work.	

1/3/18 A C Hay Capt DADOS 25th Div.

2353 Wt. W2544/1454 700,000 5/15 D. D. & L. A.D.S.S./Forms/C. 2118.

Instructions regarding War Diaries and Intelligence Summaries are contained in F. S. Regs., Part II. and the Staff Manual respectively. Title pages will be prepared in manuscript.

WAR DIARY
or
INTELLIGENCE SUMMARY.
(Erase heading not required.)

Army Form C. 2118.

DADOS
25th Division

Vol 28

Place	Date	Hour	Summary of Events and Information	Remarks and references to Appendices
Achiet-le-Petit.	1/3/18		Visited Railheads at Achiet le Grand, Bapaume & Fremicourt to obtain equipment for Machine Gun Battalion.	
	2/3/18		General Routine work.	
			Proceeded to Doullens to Canadian Stationery Dept. to obtain certain equipment for Machine Gun Coy.	
	3/3/18		General Routine Work.	
			200 tins cleaned & filled with drinking water delivered to forward dumps.	
	4.3.18.		D.A.D.O.S. left for No 14 Ordce Depot to go through short Ammn course.	
			General Routine.	
	5.3.18		General routine. Visited by DADOS 6 Divn with reference to contemplated exchange of dumps in forthcoming move.	
	6.3.18		General Routine. Received 5 Hotchkiss guns (Corps loan), and AA mtg box, for use against hostile aircraft.	

Army Form C. 2118.

WAR DIARY
or
INTELLIGENCE SUMMARY.
(Erase heading not required.)

Instructions regarding War Diaries and Intelligence Summaries are contained in F. S. Regs., Part II. and the Staff Manual respectively. Title pages will be prepared in manuscript.

Place	Date	Hour	Summary of Events and Information	Remarks and references to Appendices
Achiet le Petit	7.3	18	General Routine	
	8.3	18	General Routine. Stores visited by DAQMG	
	9.3	18	General Routine	
	10.3	18	General Routine. Prepared for move. Cancelled.	
	11.3	18	General Routine	
	12.3	18	General Routine. Stores visited by AAQMG. Prepared 240 petrol tins for holding water for issue to Pack Tport Coy	
	13.3	18	General Routine. Pack Tport Coy formed. Issued 100 Packsaddlery sets to Tport Coy, also supplied 480 galls of water in petrol tins	
	14.3	18	General Routine General Routine. Depot visited by ADOS IV Corps	
	15.3	18	General Routine, stores visited by DAQMG.	
	16.3	18	General Routine. Amalgamation of 25 A.S.C and 46 A.S. Parks	
	17.3	18	into the 25 M.T. Coy	
	18.3	18	General Routine	

2353 Wt. W2544/1454 700,000 5/15 D. D. & L. A.D.S.S./Forms/C. 2118.

Army Form C. 2118.

Instructions regarding War Diaries and Intelligence Summaries are contained in F. S. Regs., Part II. and the Staff Manual respectively. Title pages will be prepared in manuscript.

WAR DIARY
or
INTELLIGENCE SUMMARY.
(Erase heading not required.)

Place	Date	Hour	Summary of Events and Information	Remarks and references to Appendices
	19/3/18		General Routine work	
	20/3/18		Returned from Ammunition Course + arrived division on	
	21/3/18		German offensive started 4·30 a.m.	
	22/3/18 23/3/18		Ordered to stand to. Time chiefly occupied in loading + unloading stores so that guns could be obtained from Gun parks + delivered to forward area.	
	24/3/18		Moved from Achiet-le-petit to Souastre at 10. pm arrived latter place 2 a.m. morning of	
	25/3/18		Moved to Authie 8 pm and billeted with 225 Employment Coy + Salvage Coy	
	26/3/18		Moved to Hem at 12·30. Moved back to Authieule by order of DADOS at 2·30	
	27/3/18		Moved to Puchvillers at 2 pm and then to Canaples at 5·30 pm	

2353 Wt. W2544/1454 700,000 5/15 D. D. & L. A.D.S.S./Forms/C. 2118.

Instructions regarding War Diaries and Intelligence Summaries are contained in F. S. Regs., Part II. and the Staff Manual respectively. Title pages will be prepared in manuscript.

WAR DIARY
or
INTELLIGENCE SUMMARY.
(Erase heading not required.)

Army Form C. 2118.

Place	Date	Hour	Summary of Events and Information	Remarks and references to Appendices
Camples	28/3/18		All units visited under difficulties, DADOS visiting 7th Bde + 74th & 75th were visited by Chief Clerk + B Warrant Officer. Notes of principal items required, or probably required were taken + estimated indent for important stores such as M.Guns were sent in.	
	29/3/18		General work of elucidating indents + requirements & verification of such demands.	
	30/3/18		Moved to Candas at 4.30 pm. DADOS + Staff entrained at railhead at 10.15 pm. (Chief Clerk + 4 storemen proceeded to Caestre by lorry at 9.30)	
	31/3/18		Arrived at Caestre & proceeded to Merris by motor lorry. All above moves etc from 21st to date were carried out + communication had to be kept without car for DADOS which was being overhauled + no other car could be obtained. Lorries arrived at Merris 11 pm.	

2353 Wt. W2544/1454 700,000 5/15 D. D. & L. A.D.S.S./Forms/C. 2118.

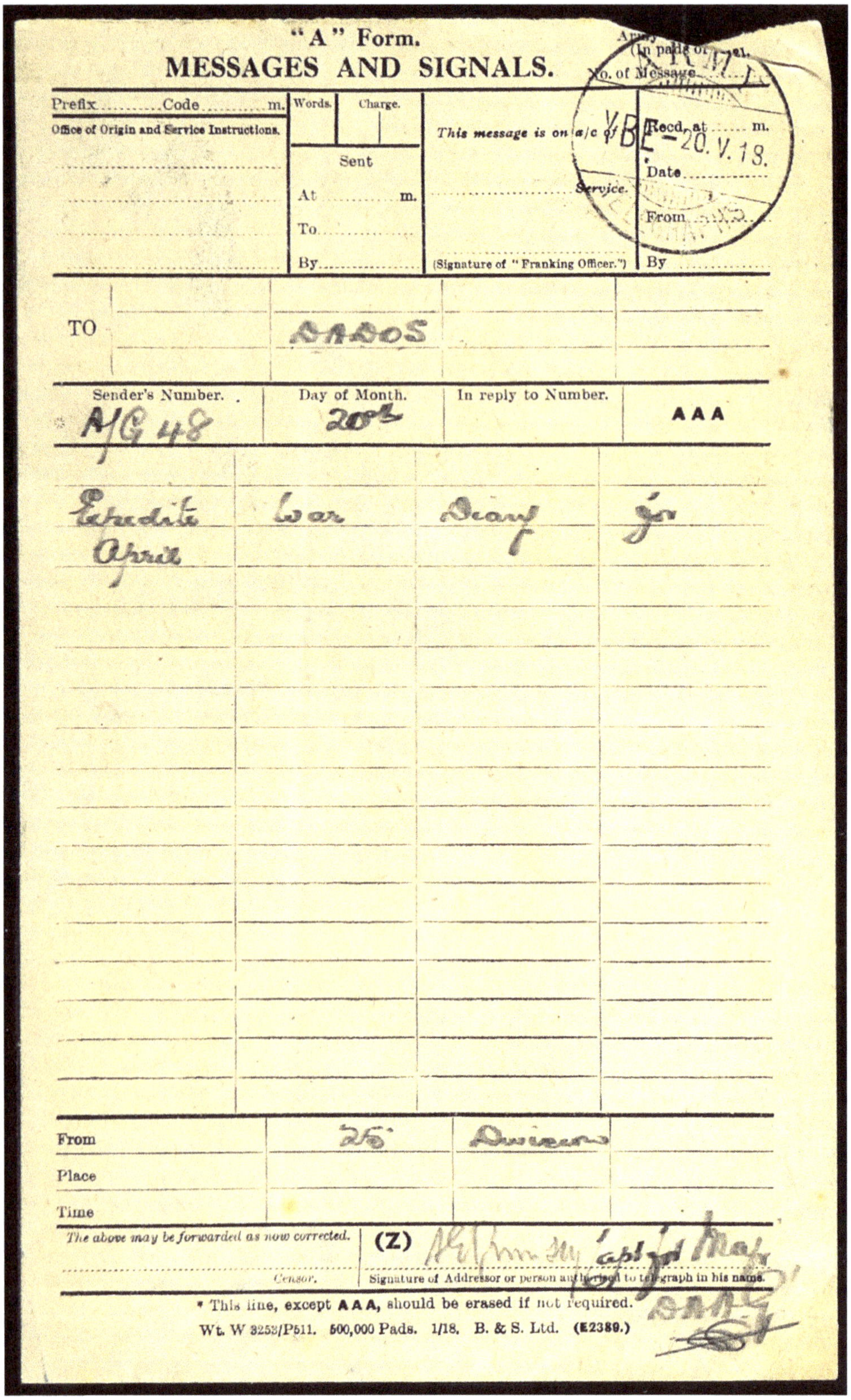

"A" Form.

MESSAGES AND SIGNALS.

Army Form C. 2121. (In pads of 100.)

No. of Message

Prefix .... Code .... m. | Words. | Charge.

Office of Origin and Service Instructions.

Sent

At .... m.

To ....

By ....

This message is on a/c of: .... Service.

(Signature of "Franking Officer.")

Recd. at .... m.

Date ....

From ....

By ....

VBE – 20. V. 18.

TO DADOS

Sender's Number.	Day of Month.	In reply to Number.	AAA
A/G 48	20th		

Expedite War Diary for April

From 25 Division

Place

Time

The above may be forwarded as now corrected. (Z)

Censor.

Signature of Addressor or person authorised to telegraph in his name. [illegible] Capt for Maj DAAG

* This line, except **AAA**, should be erased if not required.

Wt. W 3253/P511. 500,000 Pads. 1/18. B. & S. Ltd. (E2389.)

DAAG
25th Div

Herewith

A C H Taylor
Capt
DADOS

21/5/18

Instructions regarding War Diaries and Intelligence Summaries are contained in F. S. Regs., Part II. and the Staff Manual respectively. Title pages will be prepared in manuscript.

WAR DIARY
or
INTELLIGENCE SUMMARY.
(Erase heading not required.)

Army Form C. 2118.

DADOS
25th Division Vol 29

Place	Date	Hour	Summary of Events and Information	Remarks and references to Appendices
Merris.	1/4/18		100 Lewis Guns + 44 Vickers obtained from Army Gun Park to equip 7th Bde 74th Bde + M.G. Bttn.	
			8000 Blankets delivered to three brigades, MG Bttn + Pioneers.	
	2/4/18		5 six inch Newton Mortars delivered to Australian D.T.M.O.	
	3/4/18		8 3" Stokes delivered to 7th Bde T.M. Coy.	
			Moved from Merris to De Seule.	
De Seule	4/4/18		General revision + passing of indents to Base for supply. Issue of Great coats, packs etc. to complete units as far as possible.	
	5/4/18		Surplus M.Guns + parts returned to No 2 Gun Park	
	6/4/18		General Routine Work. Certain amount of clothing received for refitting purposes.	
	7/4/18		General Routine work. Large amount of stores of all kinds issued to units	

2353 Wt. W2544/1454 700,000 5/15 D. D. & L. A.D.S.S./Forms/C. 2118.

Instructions regarding War Diaries and Intelligence Summaries are contained in F. S. Regs., Part II. and the Staff Manual respectively. Title pages will be prepared in manuscript.

WAR DIARY
or
INTELLIGENCE SUMMARY.
(Erase heading not required.)

Army Form C. 2118.

DADOS
25th Div

Place	Date	Hour	Summary of Events and Information	Remarks and references to Appendices
De Seule	8/4/18		Visited 75th Field Ambulance, 3rd Worcesters, S.W. Borderers, Lancs Fusiliers.	
			Large quantity of detail stores received from Base.	
	9/4/18		Moved to Meteren. All installed by 5 am 10/4/18	
Meteren	10/4/18		Moved to Godewaersvelde. Moved completed 6 am 11/4/18	
Godwaersvelde	11/4/18		Vickers & Lewis guns delivered to units.	
	12/4/18		All surplus stores above four lorry loads returned to Base by order of AA & QMG.	
	13/4/18		Moved to Steenvoorde.	
Steenvoorde	14/4/18		DADOS moved personally to DHQ at Boeschepe & then out of direct communication with Ordnance Stores for two days.	
	15/4/18		30 Lewis & 31 Vickers guns fetched from Gun Park & delivered to Brigade.	

Instructions regarding War Diaries and Intelligence Summaries are contained in F. S. Regs., Part II. and the Staff Manual respectively. Title pages will be prepared in manuscript.

WAR DIARY
or
INTELLIGENCE SUMMARY.
(Erase heading not required.)

DADOS 25th Div.

Army Form C. 2118.

Place	Date	Hour	Summary of Events and Information	Remarks and references to Appendices
Steenvoorde	16/4/18		Stores commence to come up again from Base.	
	17/4/18		DADOS returned to Steenvoorde with Rear DHQ.	
	18/4/18		Harness, Horseshoes Wheels & other wagon parts received from Base & units wired to to draw forthwith.	
	19/4/18		Large consignment of Socks, Great coats, Shirts Wagon parts & wheels received from Base to make up divisional deficiencies	
	20/4/18		General Routine work	
Sandyhook Camp.	21/4/18		Moved to Proven area & camped at Sandyhook.	
	22/4/18		Cleared Railhead by all night work & completed move from Steenvoorde.	
Jock Camp	23/4/18		Moved to Jock Camp to make room for Div. Employment Coy at Sandyhook. S/Cond. Salter left for O.O. 9th Corps Troops taking one lorry & Brigade clerk to administer 25th Div. Artillery who is transferred to above Ordnance Officer under ADOS authority IX Corps. Car received from Workshops after 6 weeks away.	

2353 Wt. W2544/1454 700,000 5/15 D. D. & L. A.D.S.S./Forms/C. 2118.

Instructions regarding War Diaries and Intelligence Summaries are contained in F. S. Regs., Part II. and the Staff Manual respectively. Title pages will be prepared in manuscript.

WAR DIARY
or
INTELLIGENCE SUMMARY.
(Erase heading not required.)

DADOS
2nd Div

Army Form C. 2118.

Place	Date	Hour	Summary of Events and Information	Remarks and references to Appendices
Fork Camp	24/4/18		Units advised to draw available stores. Dump fairly well cleared by units.	
	25/4/18		Proceeded to Ecce + Centre to see the D.A.C. + Artillery Brigades. Could not obtain map reference of latter so phoned from 33rd D.A. to explain the transfer to D.O. IX Corps Troops.	
	26/4/18		General Routine Work. Moved to Houtkerke.	
	27/4/18 28/4/18		Move to Houtkerke completed. Made arrangements to send Winter Clothing to Railhead by lorries that delivered stores to Brigades. Many units did not make use of lorries.	
	29/4/18 30/4/18		General Routine work. A few stores arrived from base + were distributed to units. Units complete with Vickers + Lewis as far as demands shown.	

2353 Wt. W2544/1454 700,000 5/15 D. D. & L. A.D.S.S./Forms/C. 2118.

Army Form C. 2118.

Instructions regarding War Diaries and Intelligence Summaries are contained in F. S. Regs., Part II. and the Staff Manual respectively. Title pages will be prepared in manuscript.

WAR DIARY
or
INTELLIGENCE SUMMARY.
(Erase heading not required.)

DADOS
25th Division

Vol 3

Place	Date	Hour	Summary of Events and Information	Remarks and references to Appendices
HOUTKERKE	1/5/18		Equipment received from Base. Horse shoes oil + grease also distributed to units. Visited Rousbrugge Railhead + arranged to place Salvage Sgt with clerk + Storeman to receive Winter clothing etc from Divisional units.	
	2/5/18		Visited ADOS XXII Corps at Zuytpeene.	
	3/5/18		Wired to VIII Corps Troops to move 25th D.A. to me & to send back Brig. Warrant Officer with lorry & stores. Artillery apparently want large quantities of Equipment	
	4/5/18		Moved to Bambecque with DHQ + took over Office + Stores from DADOS 59th Div. Sent off lorry load of stores etc to 25th D.A.	
			Visited ADOS VIII Corps to find out + clear up delay in issues to Artillery. Found to be chiefly due to numerous changes of formation.	

2353 Wt. W2544/1454 700,000 5/15 D. D. & L. A.D.S.S./Forms/C. 2118.

Instructions regarding War Diaries and Intelligence Summaries are contained in F. S. Regs., Part II. and the Staff Manual respectively. Title pages will be prepared in manuscript.

WAR DIARY
or
INTELLIGENCE SUMMARY.
(Erase heading not required.)

Army Form C. 2118.

Place	Date	Hour	Summary of Events and Information	Remarks and references to Appendices
Bomecque	5/5/18		General Routine work. Field cookers arrived & distributed to units.	
	6/5/18		Preparation made for move. Calais Base instructed to transfer all indents to Havre & Rouen bases & to suspend all issues.	
	7/5/18		All stores with exception of offices & records consigned by rail to IX Corps Railhead.	
	8/5/18 9/5/18		} Entrained at Heidebeke.	
	10/5/18		Arrived Fere en Tardenois & proceeded to D.H.Q. at Arcis le Ponsart.	
Arcis le Ponsart	11/5/18		Visited A.D.O.S. IX Corps. Arranged new stores etc. Base wired that 11 tons clothing on rail.	
	12/5/18		General Routine work. No stores yet received in this area.	
	13/5/18		Ordered by G.O.C. to proceed to Havre Depot to go into question of outstanding stores.	

2353 Wt. W2544/1454 700,000 5/15 D. D. & L. A.D.S.S./Forms/C. 2118.

Instructions regarding War Diaries and Intelligence Summaries are contained in F. S. Regs., Part II. and the Staff Manual respectively. Title pages will be prepared in manuscript.

WAR DIARY
or
INTELLIGENCE SUMMARY.
(Erase heading not required.)

Army Form C. 2118.

Place	Date	Hour	Summary of Events and Information	Remarks and references to Appendices
Arcis le Ponsart	14/5/18		Proceeded to Havre via Paris. Purchased in latter place Red cloth, Mugs, plates and black board for Divisional School. Clothing received from Base	
	15/5/18		Arrived Havre & reported to Ordnance depot. Visited all groups & sections and noted dues out to the Division. Position of supply very satisfactory.	
	16/5/18		Picketing gear received from Base & distributed to units. Proceeded from Havre to Arcis le Ponsart.	
	17/5/18		General Routine work.	
	18/5/18		Eleven tons Stores received from Base & split up for distribution to units	
	19/5/18		Eight tons stores received — do — do —	
	20/5/18		Visited A.D.O.S. IX Corps re Gun Park Procedure. Heis trying to obtain meat safes for Divisional requirements.	
	21/5/18		General Routine Work. 12 tons stores received from Base	

Instructions regarding War Diaries and Intelligence Summaries are contained in F. S. Regs., Part II. and the Staff Manual respectively. Title pages will be prepared in manuscript.

WAR DIARY
or
INTELLIGENCE SUMMARY.
(Erase heading not required.)

Army Form C. 2118.

DADOS 35th Div

Place	Date	Hour	Summary of Events and Information	Remarks and references to Appendices
Arcis le Ponsart	22/5/18		Eight tons detail stores received from Base. Visited 7th Brigade.	
MONTIGNY	23/5/18		General Routine Work.	
	24/5/18		General Routine	
	25/5/18		General Routine. Stores visited by D.A.Q.M.G.	
	26/5/18		General Routine. 20 Tons stores received from Base including 8000 sets underclothing. Issued [?] to Div Baths.	
	27.5.18		separately [?] Dump shelled during early morning, Gas noticed, several men slightly affected. General Routine. Endeavoured to return all important stores to Base. 4 Lorry loads of stores returned to St GILLES Railhead	

Army Form C. 2118.

Instructions regarding War Diaries and Intelligence Summaries are contained in F. S. Regs., Part II. and the Staff Manual respectively. Title pages will be prepared in manuscript.

WAR DIARY
or
INTELLIGENCE SUMMARY.
(Erase heading not required.)

Place	Date	Hour	Summary of Events and Information	Remarks and references to Appendices
MONTIGNY	27/5/18		One lorry to collect stores from XI French Depôt missing with 4 men. High explosive Shrapnel over dumps continually during afternoon and evening	
	28/5/18		Left Montigny at 7.30 AM to report to HQ Division at SAVIGNY – thence ARCIS le PONSART – thence VEZILLY thence AOUGNY. DADOS returned from Leave. Moved to Goussancourt	
	29/5/18		Moved to Passy 5 AM + then to Verneuil 11 am and thence to la Chapelle at 5 pm. 16 Vickers guns delivered.	
	30/5/18		Moved to Bergues at 5 am.	
	31/5/18		Visited A.D.O.S. Corps & obtained 35 Lewis Guns at once for composite brigade	

A C Wood[illegible] Capt
DADOS

2353 Wt. W2544/1454 700,000 5/15 D. D. & L. A.D.S.S./Forms/C. 2118.

Instructions regarding War Diaries and Intelligence Summaries are contained in F. S. Regs., Part II. and the Staff Manual respectively. Title pages will be prepared in manuscript.

Army Form C. 2118.

WAR DIARY
or
INTELLIGENCE SUMMARY.
(Erase heading not required.)

June

DADOS 25th Divn

VR 31

Place	Date	Hour	Summary of Events and Information	Remarks and references to Appendices
Bergues	1/6/18		Visited ADOS IX Corps to try & obtain stores.	
	2/6/18		Large number of indents received to complete units to requirements. 50 Lewis guns drawn from Corps of which 20 given to 75th Bde.	
	3/6/18		Moved to Etoges.	
Etoges	4/6/18		Visited Railhead at Connantre with S.S.O. One truck in on	
	5/6/18		pack train with horseshoes, oil, grease equipment. Truckage system somewhat complicated. Apparently another truck for Ordnance to be collected tomorrow.	
	6/6/18		Lorries sent to railhead. Truck mentioned above still not available for offloading.	
	7/6/18		Stores received from Railhead.	
	8/6/18		8 a.m. moved to Allemant. Move completed 11.30 pm.	
Allemant	9/6/18		General Routine. Fixing up dump.	
	10/6/18		Clothing etc issued to forward Brigade.	

2353 Wt. W2544/1454 700,000 5/15 D. D. & L. A.D.S.S./Forms/C. 2118.

Instructions regarding War Diaries and Intelligence Summaries are contained in F. S. Regs., Part II. and the Staff Manual respectively. Title pages will be prepared in manuscript.

WAR DIARY
or
INTELLIGENCE SUMMARY.
(Erase heading not required.)

Army Form C. 2118.

Place	Date	Hour	Summary of Events and Information	Remarks and references to Appendices
Albert	11/6/18		13 loads stores from Base (Ground sheets, oil grease soap etc)	
			Load of stores sent to 112 Bde RFA + to 74th Bde (forward)	
	12/6/18		General Routine work. No stores at Railhead	
	13/6/18		Stores from Railhead – about 20 tons.	
	14/6/18		Moved to Pleurs. 20 tons at railhead.	
Pleurs			Visited ADOS IX Corps to arrange about Guns, Hows & Carriage	
	15/6/18		Despatched stores to 74th Bde + Artillery.	
	16/6/18		10 tons stores received from Railhead.	
			Despatched stores to 112 Bde RFA in forward area	
	17/6/18		110 Bde & 74th Bde.	
	18/6/18		ADOS called. Proceeded with him to DADOS 50th Division re stores for units being transferred to 50th Div.	
	19/6/18		Arranged with DADOS 50th to take all stores surplus to our requirements also stores that cannot be drawn by our units through lack of transport.	

WAR DIARY

or

INTELLIGENCE SUMMARY.

(Erase heading not required.)

Army Form C. 2118.

Instructions regarding War Diaries and Intelligence Summaries are contained in F. S. Regs., Part II. and the Staff Manual respectively. Title pages will be prepared in manuscript.

Place	Date	Hour	Summary of Events and Information	Remarks and references to Appendices
[illegible]	20/6/18		General Routine Work.	
	21/6/18		Arrangements for transferring stores to 50th Div	
	23/6/18		S/Cond. Smith, Storeman + clerk sent with stores to Dados 50th div. + to remain with him until all units stores recd from Base had been properly checked.	
	24/6/18		Offices + remaining stores with me despatched by rail to new destination.	
	25/6/18		Entrained to Hesdin	
	26/6/18			
	27/6/18		Arrived Hesdin and moved to Royon.	
	28/6/18		No stores received from Bases. General Routine Work	
	29/6/18		~~[illegible]~~ D.H.Q. including Dados moved to Boulogne en route for England. Left S/Cond. Salter to attend to Artillery + remaining units.	
	30/6/18		Crossed from Boulogne to Folkestone. Arriving Aldershot 7.30 pm. Act Offr	

2353 Wt. W2544/1454 700,000 5/15 D. D. & L. A.D.S.S./Forms/C. 2118.

DADOS 25 D

Vol 32

War Diary. July 1918

Mitchett Camp Aldershot.

Nothing to report for July as no stores were issued by me during this month.

9th July

Conductor C. G. Journeaux A.O.C. proceeded to Dover to report to C.O.O. for 6 months tour of duty.

Conductor G.W. Hamilton arrived to replace above W.O.

A.C.H. [illegible] Major
DADOS
25th Div

14

War Diary

~~DADOS~~ 25 D.

August 1918

VR 33

Place	Date	
Mitchell	1-8-18	Nil
	2-8-18	16 Lewis guns per Bttn despatched to units by C.O.O. Aldershot.
	3-8-18 to 12-8-18	Nothing to report. No stores issued
	13-8-18	Arrangements made for Equipment etc to be issued
	14, 15, 16	500 sets equipment, 500 Rifles, 500 Box respirators } despatched to Bttns; all signalling equipment + } – do – School of Signalling
	17-8-18 to 30-8-18	Nothing to report No stores issued

ACH [illegible]
Major
DADOS
25th Div.

DADOS 25 Division

War Diary. Sept 1918

Vol 34

Place	Date	
Antchett Camp	1-9-18 to 6-9-18	Nothing to report. No Stores issued.
	7-9-18	11th Sussex regiment commenced to draw mobilization equipment of slightly altered establishment to equip for Russia
	8-9-18 9-9-18	Equipping of Sussex completed with exception of few small items not available.
	10 11 12 13 9-18	17th Kings Liverpool Regt + 6th Yorkshire Regt completed as above with mobilization equipment together 236th Bde HQ + 236th Light T.M. Battery.
	14-9-18	Prepared to come over sea. Moved to Folkestone. (Divisional HdQ + Employment Coy only)
	15-9-18	Crossed to Boulogne.

War Diary Sept. 1918

Place	Date	
Boulogne	16-9-18	Moved to St Riquier.
St Riquier	17-9-18	Divisional details arrived from Royon district
	18-9-18	Visited Brigades and indented for urgent Stores required. A few small necessary items and 80 boxes horse shoes drawn from C.O.O Abbeville
	19-9-18 to 20-9-18	Routine work and fixing up of divisional dump.
	21-9-18 to 26-9-18	No Stores received from Havre or Rouen. Hastners sent to both bases.
	27-9-18	Moved to Henencourt
Henencourt	28-9-18	Truck of Clothing received from Rouen including 5000 prs Socks, 5000 towels + 2000 shirts all of which handed over to Divisional Employment Coy
	29-9-18	Moved to Montauban
	30-9-18	General Routine + office work

A C H Bagly Major
DADOS
25th Div.

DADOS

War Diary October 1918

Vol 35

Place	date	
Montauban	1/10/18	Moved to Combles. One truck containing missing limbers + stores of 1/5 Gloucester + 13th D.L.I received. Stores offloaded + limbers reconsigned to COO Abbeville
	3/10/18	Moved to Aizecourt. First consignment received from Havre. containing Box respirators for Divl. reserve.
Aizecourt	4/10/18	Moved to Villers-Faucon + from thence to St Emilie. Truck received from base containing Steel Helmets for exchange.
St Emilie	5/10/18	Two trucks stores received from Base.
	6/10/18	25th M G Bttn and Divisional Artillery returned to Division.
		600 Box Respirators returned to XIII Corps Troops Ordnance. 100 Camp Kettles etc to Reception Camp.
	7/10/18	B.W.O, clerk + Storeman returned with stores on Artillery rejoining.
	8/10/18	Lorry sent to 4th Army Gun Park for o/s items.
	9/10/18	Eighteen 3" Stokes Mortars + 15 Lewis M.G. drawn from 4th Army Gun Park
Estrées	10/10/18	Moved to Estrées. 12 lorry loads stores to move. One lorry of the 3 allotted broke down. Not in communication direct with Division Corps or Railhead.
	11/10/18	No stores at Railhead. Finished move from St Emilie
	12/10/18	— do — . Sent out 4 lorry loads of stores.

War Diary Oct. 1918

Place	date	
Estrees	13/10/18	L/cpl Blay proceeded to Roisel to Convoy stores to Joncourt on Light Railway. System very unsatisfactory
	14/10/18	Marquee pitched at Joncourt to receive stores off loaded from Light Rly
	15/10/18	2000 leather jerkins received + delivered to Artillery
	16/10/18	General Routine work.
	18/10/18	Moved to Maretz
Maretz.	19/10/18 } 20/10/18 }	No stores received from Base.
	21/10/18	16762 Drawers Woollen received. half given to units according to their demand + the other half to Div^n Laundry
	22/10/18	10,000 Vests + 3242 leather jerkins received from Base. Latter issued 1000 to each brigade remainder to 25th M.G. Bttn
	23/10/18 } 24/10/18 }	General Routine Work
	25/10/18	Moved to Honnechy with 17 lorry loads of stores
Honnechy	26/10/18	6000 leather Jerkins received from Base + 5100 Socks.

War Diary Oct. 1918.

Place	date	
Honnechy	27/10/18 28/10/18	General Routine work. Blankets received to complete 1 per man.
	29/10/18	Box respirators for Divn Reserve received from Base together with reserve of oil & flannelette
	30/10/18 31/10/18	All surplus underclothing despatched to Divn Baths at Honnechy

4/11/18

A C H [illegible] Major
DADOS
25th Divn

D.A.D.O.S.

War Diary. November 1918

Vol 36

Place	date	
Honnechy	1/11/18	No stores received from Base. 200 sets Service Dress collected from Corps & delivered to 75 Bde HQ
	2/11/18 } 3/11/18 }	4,300 sets of underclothing, 2000 blankets & picketing gear arrived from base. Also very pistols to complete Battalions, which were delivered to Bttns. Consignment of 900 sets of Service Dress also arrived. 300 sets being delivered to 75th Bde H.Q for certain purpose. 500 box respirators, 1500 yds flannelette, 20 galls of oil also delivered to SAA dump at Pomereuil. 1650 blankets delivered to different units under Corps Instruction.
	4/11/18	1854 shovels delivered to XIII Corps Bridging dump from where they were sent on to Pomereuil
	5/11/18	General Routine work
	6/11/18	Moved to Pomereuil with 16 lorry loads of stores
Pomereuil	7/11/18	Completed move.
	8/11/18	Collected Stores from Bellicourt Railhead. One lorry taken for duty at D.H.Q. Move to Landrecies

War Diary ~~Oct~~ November 1918

Place	date	Remarks.
Landrecies	9/11/18	Move to Landrecies continued
	10/11/18	Collected Stores from Belhcourt.
	11/11/18	General Routine work. Fourth lorry returned to me from DHQ.
	12/11/18	— do —
	13/11/18	Moved to le Cateau. 3 extra lorries attached. Stores sent up to Pioneer Bttn & 3 field Coys RE.
le Cateau	14/11/18	Move completed Visited Railhead. Vehicles not collected by unit to be consigned to [illegible] unless drawn by noon 15th inst. Units informed.
	15/11/18	Fixed up Armourers Shop & Shoemakers Shop.
	16/11/18	General Routine work.
	17/11/18	Clothing & Boots sent up to Pioneers &, Field Coys RE.
	18/11/18 19/11/18 20/11/18	General Routine & Office work.

War Diary Nov. 1918.

Place	Date	Remarks
le Cateau	21/11/18	Consignment of clothing + boots received from Base
	22/11/18	200 pairs of boots handed over to 9th Corps Troops.
	23/11/18	6000 blankets received + issued to infantry
	24/11/18	6500 blankets received. All units completed to 2 blankets per man.
	25th to 30th	General Routine work. No stores received from Base.
	30th	Moved to Avesnes lez Aubert.

[illegible] Major
DADOS
25th Divn

War Diary (December 1918)

DADOS.
25th Divn

VS 36

PLACE	DATE	REMARKS
Avesnes les Aubert	1/12/18	Move from le Cateau completed.
	2/12/18 3/12/18	Preparing storage + Shops.
	4/12/18	Visited Railhead at St Aubert. No stores yet arrived since 24/11/18.
	5/12/18	Visited O.O XIII Corps troops No. 3 at St Aubert with AA + DAQMG Visited 2nd, 3rd, Guards + 6th Corps Reception Camp to arrange transfer to
	6/12/18	Visited 62nd + 25th Div! Reception Camps at Cambrai
	7/12/18	Visited OO XIII Corps troops No 3 + obtained statistics of stores due to reception Camps. Visited Solesmes to obtain whereabouts of 5000 blankets; also called on 76th + 75th Field Ambulances to arrange stock of clothing etc. in Divisional Rest Station.
	8/12/18	Visited DDOS Corps
	9/12/18	obtained 2000 blankets from O.O. XIII Corps Troops No. 1. for Reception Camps + to complete Draft of Division.

War Diary (December 1918)

Place	Date	Remarks.
Avesnes-lez-Aubert	10/12/18	Truck of horseshoes received from Havre.
	11/12/18	65th Army Field Artillery Bde attached to me for Ordnance.
	12/12/18	General Routine Work.
	13/12/18	Lorries sent by XIII Corps to Havre & Rouen to bring stores from those bases. Boots especially urgent as none have been received for nearly a month due to shortage of railway ~~[illegible]~~ trucks.
	14/12/18 15/12/18 16/12/18	General Routine work.
	17/12/18	Truck received with small consignment of clothing
	18/12/18 19/12/18	3 Lorries returned from Rouen with clothing, Grindery & a few boots. 1 Truck from Rouen advised & 1 truck from Havre.
	20/12/18	

War Diary (December 1918)

Place	Date	Remarks
Nesnes Puy Aubert	21/12/18	General Routine work. Issues to units of stores available.
	22/12/18	5 lorries returned from Havre with Picketing Gear, Pallasses, Stable necessaries + Detail stores.
	23/12/18	1 lorry from Havre with similar stores.
	24/12/18	Truck received from Rouen with 800 boots, towels + shirts for laundry + Small kit. No size 6 boots two F.S boots received. 800 pairs of boots still due to division – and are urgently required.
	25/12/18	Two trucks stores received from Havre
	26/12/18 } 27/12/18 }	General issues of all stores made to units. Base changed to Calais from Havre + Rouen.
	28/12/18	Pallasses sent out to brigades for distribution.
	29/12/18	Lorry despatched to Calais to bring all boots due to Divn.
	30/12/18	Four trucks received with 3rd blanket per man for division One truck received from Havre.
	31/12/18	74 Bde units moving, all completed 3rd Blanket except A.&C. Coy.

[illegible] A-DOS 31/12/18

War Diary January 1919

DADOS 25

Vol 38

PLACE	DATE	REMARKS.
Avesnes lesAubert	1st	General Routine work
	2nd	Trucks advised from New Base (Calais)
	3rd	Lorry returned from Calais with Boots + Grindery. Still no size 6 + 7 available at Base. (Division about 400 pairs short in these sizes).
	4th	Truck of Oil, paint grease picketing gear received.
	5th	Division completed with 3 blankets per man.
	6th	Stores sent out to 7th + 74th Bdes.
	7th	General Office + Routine work
	8th	Truck of General Stores received from Base
	9th	Truck of Clothing + Boots — do —
	10th	Truck of Table + forms received from O.O. Army Troops.
		33 Chairs received from O.O XIII Corps Troops.

War Diary (January 1919)

Place	Date	Remarks
Avesnes les Aubert	11/1/19	Visited O.O. XIII Corps Troops No 3. reference return of Stores tents etc
	12/1/19	Truck of Stores received from Base.
	13/1/19	Stores sent out to 7th & 74th Bdes & all units out of horse transport distance
	14/1/19	Boots (less sizes 6 & 7) received from Base.
	15/1/19	General Routine work.
	16/1/19	Stores delivered to units
	17/1/19	General Office work
	18/1/19	1500 paillasses received and
	19/1/19	distributed according to Divisional instructions.

War Diary (January 1919)

Place	Date	Remarks
Avesnes les Aubert	20/1/19	Two trucks advised from Base
	21/1/19	General Routine work
	22/1/19	One truck advised from Base.
	23/1/19	XIII Corps Animal Collecting Station at Masnieres formed.
	24/1/19	Two trucks received from Base
	25/1/19	Urgent stores for Masnieres Collecting Station sent out also Stores for 7th + 74th Bdes.
	26/1/19	Visited ADOS XIII Corps
	27/1/19	Visited Animal Collecting Station at Masnieres.
	28/1/19	Truck received from Base (oil grease etc). Lamps 7S for distribution received from OO XIII Corps Troops to be distributed according to "Q" instruction
	29/1/19	Visited 7th + 74th Bdes. H.Q. also Durham Light Infantry Bttn + Sherwood Foresters.

War Diary. Jan 1918.

Place	date	Remarks.
Avesnes le Aubert	30/1/19	General Routine work.
	31/1/19	Truck advised from Calais.

31/1/19

[signature] ~~Maj~~ DADOS

AE 156

The
AA + QMG.
25th Division.

Enclosed [illegible] to War Diary for February 1919.

1/4/19

[illegible] Lt
for DADOS 25th Div.

War Diary (February 1919)

Vol 39

Place	Date	Remarks
Avesnes les Aubert	1/2/19	Visited Cambrai to fix site for dump during Thaw precautions.
	2/2/19	Visited ADOS XIII Corps.
	3/2/19	Truck received from Calais. (Boots, Cogs, picketing gear & Clothing)
	4/2/19	Stores sent out to the three brigades. Proceeded to Solesmes to find site for handing in of surplus stores on demobilization of units, as St Aubert site not convenient.
	5/2/19	Visited ADOS XIII Corps.
	6/2/19	Capt Hall RG 8th Royal Sussex Regt attached for duty to be reported on as suitable for RAOC. Truck received from Calais. Visited ADOS XIII Corps.
	7/2/19	General Routine work. Lorry sent to DO XIII Corps troops No 2 at Busigny to obtain any stores surplus to meet divl. demand

War Diary. (Feb 1919)

Place	Date	Remarks.
Avesnes les Aubert	8/2/19	Proceeded to Cambrai with A.D.O.S. XIII Corps to fix site for Intermediate Collecting Station.
	9/2/19	No Stores received or issued.
	10/2/19	Truck of Stores received from Calais (Boots, Horseshoes etc)
	11/2/19	Truck of Stores received from Calais (Clothing, picketing gear etc)
	12/2/19	Stores sent out to 3 Brigades.
	13/2/19	No Stores received
	14/2/19	Truck of boots, grindery etc received from Base.
	15/2/19	Thaw precaution imposed. Authority obtained from Corps to run two lorries to Cambrai for Truck of Stores arrived from Calais.
	16/2/19	Boots despatched by car to 20th Manchesters + 9th Devons.

War Diary (Feb 1919)

Place	Date	Remarks
Avesnes-les-Aubert	17/2/19	Truck of Stores arrived & cleared to dump at Cambrai annexe.
	18/2/19	General Routine work
	19/2/19	Visited A.D.O.S. XIII Corps. Truck received from Railhead & stores dumped at Annexe dump.
	20/2/19	Thaw restrictions removed. All stores cleared from Annexe dump to Avesnes

www.ingramcontent.com/pod-product-compliance
Lightning Source LLC
Chambersburg PA
CBHW081422160426
43193CB00013B/2175
9781474513289